SCHOLASTIC

Word Work & Spelling

Graphic Organizers & Mini-Lessons

Grades 2–4

Dottie Raymer

New York • Toronto • London • Auckland • Sydney
Mexico City • New Delhi • Hong Kong • Buenos Aires

Teaching Resources

Acknowledgments

To Jennifer Jacobson for creating this series and inviting me along on the ride.

Edited by Kathleen Hollenbeck
Cover design by Maria Lilja
Interior design by Holly Grundon
Interior illustrations by Teresa Anderko

ISBN-13: 978-0-439-57292-7
ISBN-10: 0-439-57292-4

Published by Scholastic Inc.

Printed in the U.S.A.

1 2 3 4 5 6 7 8 9 10 40 15 14 13 12 11 10 09 08

Contents

Introduction 4

Connections to the Standards 6

References and Additional Resources 7

Mini-Lessons

Word Vines *(comparing sound and spelling patterns)* 8

Logo Rhymes *(identifying spelling patterns that rhyme)* 10

Egg Match-Ups *(recognizing word parts)* 12

Spinning Spelling Patterns *(developing phonemic awareness)* 14

Odd Man Out *(recognizing sound-spelling patterns)* 16

Goal! *(recognizing sound-spelling patterns)* 18

"Mathemagical" Words *(forming contractions)* 20

Syllable Caterpillar *(recognizing syllables in words)* 22

Compound Word Puzzle *(recognizing compound words)* 24

Homophone Clues *(differentiating homophones and easily confused words)* 26

Skyscraper Spelling *(using spelling strategies)* 28

Spelling Survey Says…! *(grouping words by spelling patterns)* 30

Special Spelling Secret *(recognizing spelling patterns)* 32

Outlaw Words *(creating mnemonics for difficult words)* 34

Seeing Suffixes *(adding suffixes)* 36

Word Tower *(adding affixes to root words)* 38

Word Part Bicycle *(identifying prefixes, suffixes, and root words)* 40

Flowering Roots *(understanding relationships among words)* 42

Word World *(using spelling strategies)* 44

Branching Out *(examining word structure)* 46

Introduction

Welcome to *Word Work & Spelling Graphic Organizers and Mini-Lessons*! Designed for flexible use, these 20 graphic organizers help students explore spelling patterns, word structure, and strategies to help strengthen their skills in spelling, reading, and writing.

Why Teach Spelling?

Every teacher has heard—or even said—statements like those in the box below. Even more frustrating are the experiences that seem to support the statements: students who can't seem to remember the spelling of the simplest words; others who ace every spelling test but consistently misspell the very same words in their writing. No wonder teachers might think spellers must be born, not made, and that attempting to teach spelling may not be worth valuable classroom time.

Recent research has shown that there *are* very good reasons for teaching spelling—reasons that reach far beyond just "getting it right" or double-checking the spell-check on the computer.

> "Some people are just born spellers."
>
> "I've been a terrible speller all my life."
>
> "My son gets hundreds on his spelling tests, but you should see his compositions! He's just being lazy."

- Spelling instruction strengthens reading skills. The awareness of sound-letter correspondences, spelling patterns, and word structure that students learn and practice in spelling instruction are the same skills students need to become proficient readers.
- Spelling instruction enhances vocabulary development. As students learn how spellings and meanings of words are related, they develop strategies for figuring out the meanings of unfamiliar words.
- Spelling instruction supports the writing process. Poor spelling can hinder the thinking and organizational skills that are key to the writing process. Spelling must be reasonably automatic in order to encourage the flow of ideas. When students use only words they know how to spell or frequently pause to figure out spellings, they may limit or lose track of ideas they wish to express.
- Spelling instruction develops critical thinking skills. As students focus on words, they learn to compare and contrast, draw conclusions, make generalizations, and look for exceptions in how words are spelled.

Why Use Graphic Organizers to Teach Spelling?

Graphic organizers provide schemata: a way of structuring information or arranging key concepts into a pattern, enhancing comprehension and imparting useful learning strategies (Bromley et al., 1995)—all of which are essential for spelling retention. Organizers offer students an efficient, interactive way to connect their learning to new words and contexts, represent and clarify complex ideas, display their thinking, and monitor their use of learning strategies.

Research has shown that graphic organizers help students to:

- connect prior knowledge to new information (Guastello, 2000), which comes in handy when applying learned spelling rules to larger, more complex words.
- integrate language and thinking in an organized format (Bromley et al, 1995).
- engage in mid- to high-level thinking along Bloom's Taxonomy with regard to comprehension, analysis, and synthesis (Dodge, 2005). Organizers help reinforce critical thinking skills by

requiring students to sort and categorize words, analyze similarities and differences, and make inferences and generalizations based on their analysis.

How to Use This Book

The organizers in this book can be used in any order and lend themselves well to many forms of teaching: pre- and post-assessment, preparation for spelling lessons or writing assignments, and mini-lessons. They are suitable for use with the whole class, small groups, or individual students, and are ideal for homework or guided cooperative learning groups.

Each organizer targets a different skill or combination of skills, which is shown on each lesson page. At the top of the page, a purpose states the uses and benefits of the activity, and the suggestion for introducing the lesson helps set the stage and pique student interest. Step-by-step directions provide a guide for demonstrating how to use and complete the organizer. Also included is a helpful management tip, which recommends one or more specific ways to use the graphic organizer, and an activity that lets you take students a step further by building on the skills and strategies covered in the lesson or by using the organizer for a different purpose. Finally, a literature link is provided to help you connect the targeted words or concept in the lesson to a particular reading selection.

Using a Graphic Organizer

Select the graphic organizer that best suits your instructional needs. Then follow these suggestions to prepare and use the organizer with students.

- **Test It.** Before using an organizer, give it a "trial run" on your own to experience the process firsthand. This will allow you to see how well the organizer works with the selected words or concept. Make any modifications necessary to best meet the needs of your students (Egan, 1999).
- **Present It.** Determine the best method for presenting the graphic organizer. You might make a photocopy for use as a transparency on the overhead projector, or distribute paper copies to students to complete as you model its use. Keep a supply of frequently used organizers on hand for students to use independently.
- **Model It.** Research has shown that graphic organizers are most effective when the teacher presents and models the organizer first for the whole group (Bowman et al., 1998). To ensure greatest success, model the use of each organizer with the whole class before asking students to complete it independently.

Helpful Hints for Success

- Model the use of the organizer so that students will gain a clear understanding of its purpose and how to complete it.
- Choose words wisely. Use those that teach spelling patterns or principles—and that you know most students can read. Also, encourage students to select words to use on the organizers. This will reinforce their curiosity and awareness of the words they encounter.
- When discussing words, "walk and chalk." Saying and writing words simultaneously reinforces students' awareness of the sound-spelling connection.
- When analyzing words during a mini-lesson, "think out loud." This will allow students to recognize and apply your strategies for spelling difficult words.

* Create a word-rich environment. Use word walls, have students keep word journals, and provide them with word games and puzzles. Reinforce and share students' excitement about discovering new word knowledge.
* Provide adhesive note strips so students can mark unfamiliar or interesting words in the articles and books they read.
* Invite students to work together in pairs or groups to complete the organizers. This way they can pool their knowledge, share views, and build a more thorough understanding of word definitions, relationships, and concepts.

Assessing Student Performance

Graphic organizers allow you to assess a student's understanding of spelling concepts and word structure at a glance. You can use the organizers in this book to determine what students know, the depth of their understanding, what they need to know, and the connections they have made. For example, after completing Special Spelling Secret (page 32), you can have students identify words in their reading materials and environment that follow the spelling rule discovered on the organizer. Students can also use graphic organizers to assess their own learning.

Graphic organizers are a performance-based model of assessment and are ideal for including in student portfolios, as they require students to demonstrate both their grasp of the concept and their reasoning.

Connections to the Standards

This book is designed to support you in meeting the following language arts standards outlined by Mid-continent Research for Education and Learning (McREL), an organization that collects and synthesizes national and state standards.

Uses grammatical and mechanical conventions in written compositions.

* Spells high frequency, commonly misspelled, and phonetically regular words appropriate to grade level.
* Spells basic short, long, and r-controlled vowels and consonant blend patterns.
* Uses initial consonant substitution to spell related words.
* Uses contractions, compounds, roots, suffixes, prefixes, and syllable constructions to spell words.
* Uses a dictionary and other resources to spell words appropriate to grade level.

Uses the general skills and strategies of the reading process.

* Uses common letter/sound relationships, beginning and ending consonants, vowel sounds, vowel patterns, blends, and word patterns to decode unknown words.
* Uses complex word families, syllabication, root words, prefixes, suffixes, compound words, spelling patterns, and contractions to decode unknown words.

Kendall, J. S. & Marzano, R. J. (2004). *Content knowledge: A compendium of standards and benchmarks for K-12 education*. Aurora, CO: Mid-continent Research for Education and Learning. Online database: http://www.mcrel.org/standards-benchmarks/

References and Additional Resources

Bell, K. & Caspari, A. (May 2002). "Strategies for improving nonfiction reading comprehension." An Action Research Project; Saint Xavier University & Skylight Professional Development. Chicago, IL.

Bowman, L. A., Carpenter, J. & Paone, R. (1998). "Using graphic organizers, cooperative learning groups, and higher order thinking skills to improve reading comprehension." M.A. Action Research Project, Saint Xavier University. Chicago, IL.

Boyle, J. R. & Weishaar, M. (1997). "The effects of expert-generated versus student-generated cognitive organizers on the reading comprehension of students with learning disabilities." *Learning Disabilities Research and Practice, 12* (4), 228–235.

Bromley, K., Irwin-De Vitis, L. & Modlo, M. (1995). *Graphic organizers: Visual strategies for active learning.* New York: Scholastic.

Chall, J. S. (1983). *Stages of reading development.* New York: McGraw Hill.

Chang, K. E., Sung, Y. T. & Chen, I. D. (2002). "The effects of concept mapping to enhance text comprehension and summarization." *Journal of Experimental Education, 71* (1), 5–24.

Dodge, J. (2005). *Differentiation in action.* New York: Scholastic.

Dreher, M. J. (2003). "Motivating struggling readers by tapping the potential of information books." *Reading and Writing Quarterly: Overcoming Learning Difficulties, 19* (1), 25–38.

Duke, N. K. & Bennett-Armistead, V. S. (2003). *Reading & writing informational text in the primary grades: Research-based practices*. New York: Scholastic.

Egan, M. (1999). "Reflections on effective use of graphic organizers." *Journal of Adolescent and Adult Literacy, 42* (8), 641.

Guastello, E. F. (2000). "Concept mapping effects on science-content comprehension of low-achieving inner-city seventh graders." *Remedial and Special Education, 21* (6), 356.

Moore, D. & Readence, J. (1984). "A quantitative and qualitative review of graphic organizer research." *Journal of Educational Research, 78* (1), 11–17.

Pardo, L. S. (2004) "What every teacher needs to know about comprehension." *Reading Teacher, 58* (3), 272–280.

Stead, T. (2006). *Reality checks: Teaching reading comprehension with nonfiction K-5*. Portland, ME: Stenhouse.

Yopp, R. H. & Yopp, H. K. (2000). "Sharing informational text with young children." *Reading Teacher, 53 (5)*, 410–423.

Skill

- Comparing Sound and Spelling Patterns
- Developing Phonemic Awareness
- Identifying Rhyming Words

Management Tip

While modeling the use of this organizer on the overhead projector, have students complete their own copies of it.

Literature Link

A Year Down Yonder by Richard Peck (Puffin, 2000).

When Mary Alice went to live with her formidable Grandma for a year, she never expected to find adventure and love in the small Illinois town.

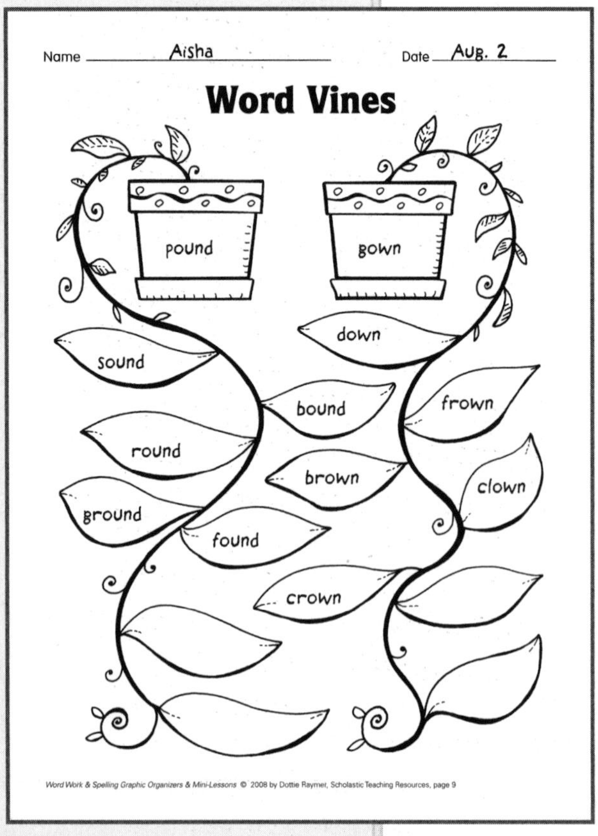

Name Aisha
Date Aug. 2
Word Vines
pound
gown
down
sound
bound
frown
round
brown
clown
ground
found
crown
Word Work & Spelling Graphic Organizers & Mini-Lessons © 2008 by Dottie Raymer, Scholastic Teaching Resources, page 9

Word Vines

Purpose

Students apply their knowledge of how words *sound* (rhyming sounds) and how they *look* (spelling patterns) to spell new words.

Introducing the Activity

Tell students that although English seems to be a quirky language, full of exceptions, most word spellings do follow regular patterns. They may be surprised to discover that they often know more about word spellings than they realize. Then explain that in this lesson, students will rely on how words sound and look—as well as what they already know—to unlock clues about spelling.

Using the Graphic Organizer

1. Distribute copies of the graphic organizer. Select two key words that share an identical sound or spelling pattern and write these on the flowerpots. For example, you might use *pound* and *gown* to represent the identical sound made by *ou* and *ow* in these words. Have students copy the words onto their organizers.
2. Discuss the targeted sounds and the spelling differences in the words. Talk about what is the same (vowel sounds) and different (spelling) about the words.
3. Encourage students to brainstorm other words that follow the sound or spelling pattern in each word. Have them fill in the leaves on each vine with words that fit the pattern of the word on each flowerpot.
4. Invite students to share their words with the class. Later have them complete the organizer using other words with targeted sound or spelling patterns.

Taking It Further

Have pairs or small groups list words that share the same vowel sound but have different spellings. Then invite them to create their own word vines from green construction paper, using words from their list.

Name ______________________________ Date ______________

Word Vines

Logo Rhymes

Purpose

Students use logos and familiar words to create word family lists.

Introducing the Activity

Most students can recognize, read, and spell the names of familiar logos and products they encounter each day. Discuss what logos are and why companies create them. Then invite students to recall—and point out—popular logos that appear on clothing, beauty products, computers, and other common items.

Using the Graphic Organizer

1. Display a familiar product or logo with a name that contains a common spelling pattern (or word family ending), such as a shampoo called *Super Shine*. Write the name in the box on a tag on the graphic organizer.
2. Help students identify the common spelling pattern in the logo, for example, "ine" in *Shine*. Then underline that spelling pattern.
3. Ask volunteers to name words that rhyme with the target word. Write their responses, such as *fine, line,* and *pine* on the tag. Then circle the group of letters in each word that rhymes with the targeted spelling pattern.
4. Ask: *Is the rhyming part of each word spelled the same? Which words contain different spelling patterns from the targeted word?* Mark each word that has a different spelling pattern. Explain that rhyming words often belong to the same word family, but different spelling patterns may also occur in words that rhyme.
5. Distribute copies of the organizer. Then write two logo or product names on the board. Have students use the words to complete the organizer. Afterward, have them share and discuss their responses.

Taking It Further

Provide two different logos or brand names and a selection of words that rhyme with each one. Have students sort the words according to spelling patterns.

Skill

- Identifying Spelling Patterns That Rhyme
- Comparing Spelling Patterns
- Making Generalizations

Management Tip

Have students find logos and brand names in sales, newspaper, and magazine ads to use on this organizer.

Literature Link

Amelia Works It Out by Marissa Moss (Pleasant Company Publications, 2000).

Since her mother refused to buy her the name-brand shoes that everyone else is wearing, Amelia schemes ways to earn money so she can buy them herself.

Name Jorge
Date Aug. 27
Logo Rhymes
Super Shine
line
pine
fine
dine
mine
Puff Pillow
row
hoe
toe
blow
BO
Word Work & Spelling Graphic Organizers & Mini-Lessons © 2008 by Dottie Raymer, Scholastic Teaching Resources, page 11

Name ______________________ Date ______________

Logo Rhymes

Egg Match-Ups

Skill

- Recognizing Word Parts
- Creating New Words
- Making Spelling Generalizations

Management Tip

After students complete this organizer independently, have them group their words by common endings and then share their lists with the class.

Literature Link

The Perfect Nest by Catherine Friend (Candlewick, 2007).

Jack, a farm cat, builds a perfect nest, hoping to lure a chicken into it to lay a perfect egg so he can make a perfect omelet.

Name Omar Date Sept. 4

Egg Match-Ups

plant chant chore
chair mop chop
stop store plop
more stair

pl | ant | ch | air
st | op | m | ore

Word Work & Spelling Graphic Organizers & Mini-Lessons © 2008 by Dottie Raymer, Scholastic Teaching Resources, page 13

Purpose

Students mix and match word parts to spell new words.

Introducing the Activity

Write *pair* and *hot* on the board and draw a pair of egg halves for each word. Work with students to divide each word into two parts—the letter that makes up its initial sound and its word family ending. Write each part on an egg half. Then ask students to create new words by putting together the sounds represented on the eggs. Did they come up with *pot* and *hair?* Explain that in this activity, they will use parts of different words to create and spell new words.

Using the Graphic Organizer

1. Select four words that begin with a consonant (or consonant blend) and have a word family ending. Try to choose words for which some of the word parts can be interchanged to create new words, such as *plant, chair, stop,* and *more.* Write the words on the board.
2. Distribute copies of the graphic organizer. Ask students to write the words on the nest, leaving space to add more words later.
3. Work with students to divide each word into its initial and word ending parts. Have them write the parts of each word on a pair of egg halves.
4. Instruct students to work with the word parts on the eggs to create as many new words as possible, such as *chant, store, mop, stair, chore,* and so on. Have them write each new word on the nest.
5. Invite students to share their new words with the class.

Taking It Further

You might have students cut out the eggs after they write the word parts in them. Then they can manipulate the different egg halves to create new words.

Name ______________________________ Date ______________

Egg Match-Ups

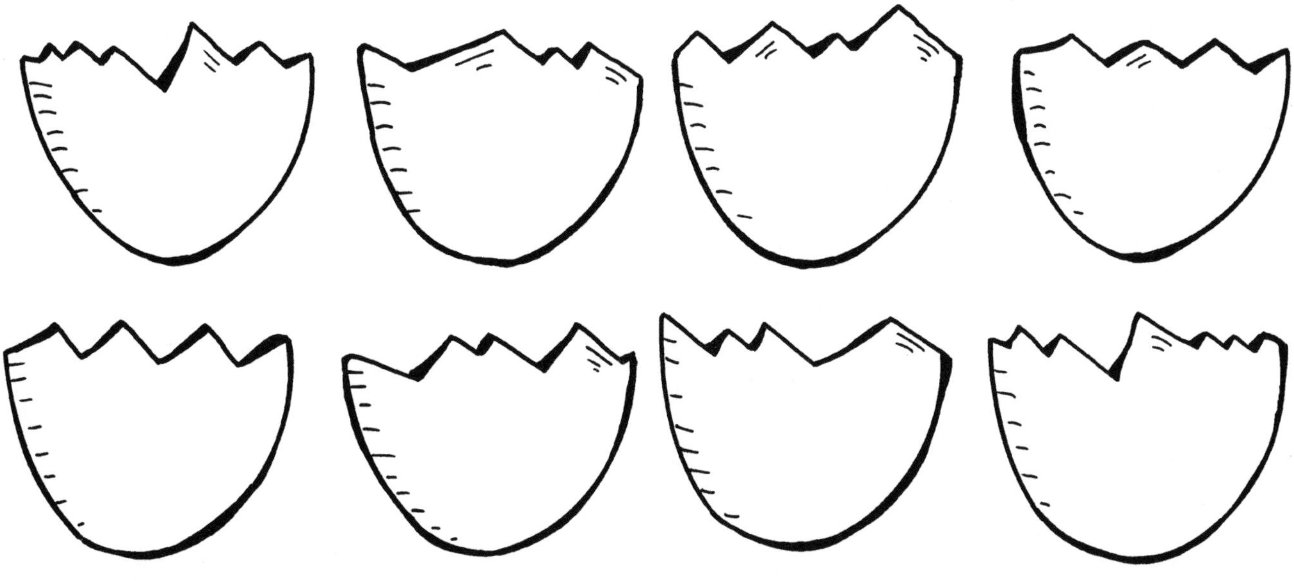

Spinning Spelling Patterns

Skill

- Developing Phonemic Awareness
- Using Spelling Patterns
- Using Letter-Sound Associations

Management Tip

After modeling how to use this organizer, invite students to brainstorm words in pairs or groups to complete the activity.

Literature Link

Miss Spider's Tea Party by David Kirk (Scholastic Press, 1994).

All the insects flee from Miss Spider until they learn of her kindness to a rain-soaked moth.

Purpose

Students brainstorm words that are spelled with targeted phonemic elements.

Introducing the Activity

Write four different phonemic elements or common spelling patterns on the board (such as *at, it, et,* and *ut*). Explain that each of these patterns can be found in a variety of words. Invite students to name words that contain the patterns, writing their responses under the appropriate ones. Talk about the targeted pattern in the words, as well as other letter-sound associations used when spelling and saying them. Then tell students they will use the graphic organizer to create their own lists of words that contain targeted spelling patterns.

Using the Graphic Organizer

1. Distribute copies of the graphic organizer. Write on the board four phonemic elements or spelling patterns that you want students to work with, such as *ai, ea, oa,* and *ee.*
2. Have students write each pattern in a top section of the spider web.
3. Ask students to brainstorm words they know that are spelled with each pattern. Instruct them to write a different word in each section of the spider web under the corresponding spelling pattern. Challenge them to try to fill in the entire web.
4. Invite students to share their words with the class. Discuss the spelling of each, referring to a dictionary to validate any questionable spellings.

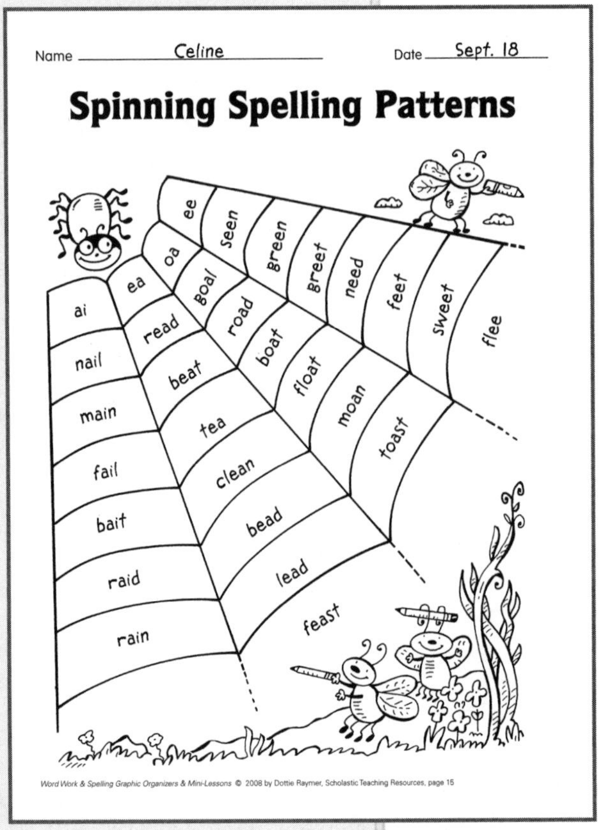
Name Celine
Date Sept. 18
Spinning Spelling Patterns
ai
nail
main
fail
bait
raid
rain
ea
read
beat
tea
clean
bead
lead
feast
oa
goal
road
boat
float
moan
toast
ee
seen
green
greet
need
feet
sweet
flee
Word Work & Spelling Graphic Organizers & Mini-Lessons © 2008 by Dottie Raymer, Scholastic Teaching Resources, page 15

Taking It Further

To expand vocabulary along with spelling skills, ask students to write commonly used words such as *cold, big, mad,* and *fast* in the top sections of the web. Then have them write synonyms for each word to complete the web.

Name ____________________ Date ____________

Spinning Spelling Patterns

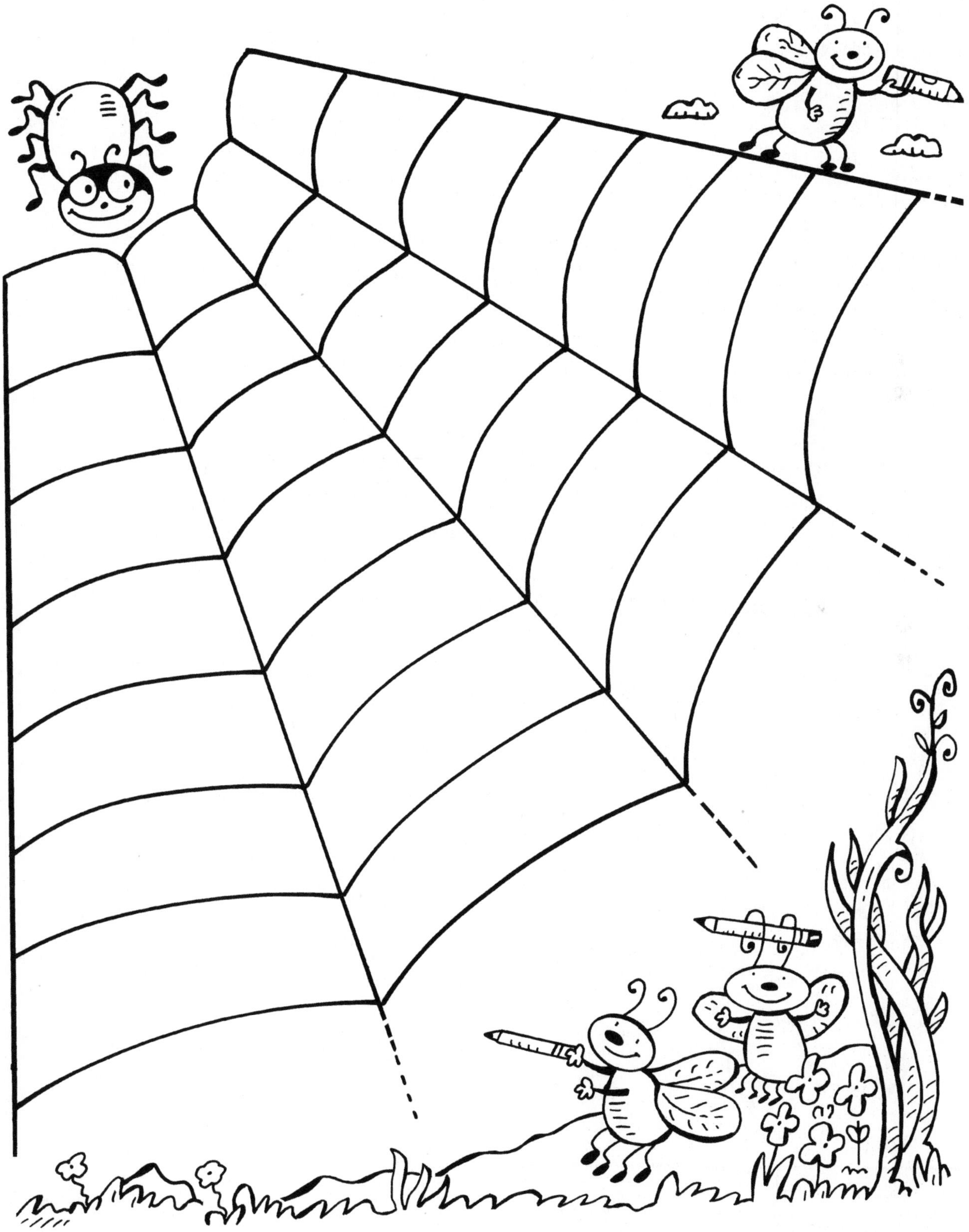

Odd Man Out

Purpose

Students compare and categorize words to develop generalizations about sound-spelling correspondences.

Introducing the Activity

Invite students to name several word family endings, such as *ed, ag,* and *op*. Draw a chart on the board and write these in the top columns. Then ask students to name words that belong to each word family and identify which column they should be listed under.

Using the Graphic Organizer

1. Select three categories of words with somewhat similar sound or spelling patterns (for example, those spelled with short *e, ea,* and *ee*). List words for each category on the board in random order. Also include one "odd man out"—a similar word that doesn't fit any of the categories. For example, *bread* has the same spelling pattern as *bead* and *plead,* but is pronounced differently.

2. Distribute copies of the graphic organizer. Explain that some words on the list are alike in some way. Then identify two words and explain how they are alike. Have students write these words on a pair of cards. Ask them to find other words from the list that are similar and write these on the other pairs of cards.

3. After filling in the card pairs, ask students to find the "odd man out"—a word that doesn't make a pair with any other word on the list. Have them write that word on the single card.

4. Invite students to share their word pairs with the class. Then discuss each word that students identified as the "odd man out." Ask: *Does this word look or sound like any other word on the list? Why do you think it's the "odd man out?"* Help them understand why they did or did not choose the correct word for this card.

Taking It Further

Invite students to create their own word pair cards to use in familiar card games such as Concentration and Go Fish.

Skill

- Recognizing Sound-Spelling Patterns
- Developing Phonemic Awareness
- Identifying Differences in Sound-Spelling Patterns

Management Tip

After students become familiar with this organizer, have them choose and form categories with their own sets of words.

Literature Link

Bread and Jam for Frances by Russell Hoban (HarperTrophy, 1993).

The picky eater Frances insists on eating only bread and jam at every meal.

Name Liam
Date Oct. 10
Odd Man Out
feed
seed
bed
red
bead
plead
bread
Word Work & Spelling Graphic Organizers & Mini-Lessons © 2008 by Dottie Raymer, Scholastic Teaching Resources, page 17

Name ______________________________ Date ________________

Odd Man Out

Skill

- Recognizing Sound-Spelling Patterns
- Differentiating Sound-Spelling Patterns
- Using Visual Memory to Spell

Management Tip

Demonstrate how to use this organizer on the overhead projector.

Literature Link

The Little Old Lady Who Was Not Afraid of Anything by Linda Williams (HarperTrophy, 1988).

While heading home through a dark forest, a little old lady meets with articles of clothing that have a life of their own!

Goal!

Purpose

Students compare words that sound the same but contain different spelling patterns.

Introducing the Activity

Explain that writers often rely on their memory of how words look to tell whether they are spelled correctly. To demonstrate how visual memory helps aid spelling, make a list of familiar words, intentionally misspelling a few with similar sound-spelling patterns (such as *right, light, bight, kite, write, fite*). Ask students to identify all the words that "look right." Then discuss each word's spelling and why it is or isn't correct.

Using the Graphic Organizer

1. Display two words that contain different spelling patterns for the same sound, such as *paid* and *made*. Underline the same-sounding spelling pattern in each word (*aid* and *ade*).
2. Write each spelling pattern at the top of the chart. Also write each one on a goalpost on the graphic organizer.
3. Have students name words that contain the sound for the two spelling patterns. Write each word in both columns of the T-chart, using the spelling pattern for that column to spell the word (for example, *graid* and *grade*). Then have students look at each pair of words. Ask: *Which spelling looks right for this word?*
4. After students agree on a spelling, have a volunteer look up the word in a dictionary. Record the word on the side of the field that corresponds to its spelling pattern, writing it on the line nearest the 50-yard line. Continue, filling in words toward each goal until one side of the field is filled or all the word choices have been exhausted.
5. Distribute copies of the organizer for students to complete using a new pair of words.

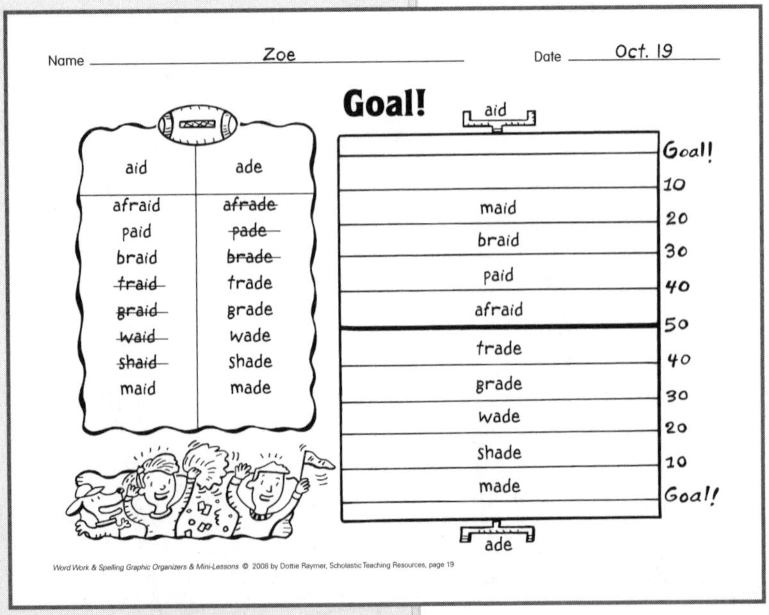
Name Zoe
Date Oct. 19
Goal!
aid
ade
afraid
afrade
paid
pade
braid
brade
fraid
trade
graid
grade
waid
wade
shaid
shade
maid
made
Goal!
10
20
30
40
50
maid
braid
paid
afraid
trade
grade
wade
shade
made
ade
Word Work & Spelling Graphic Organizers & Mini-Lessons © 2008 by Dottie Raymer, Scholastic Teaching Resources, page 19

Taking It Further

Invite groups of three to complete the organizer. Ask one student to record words on the chart, another on the football field, and a third to verify the spellings.

Name ______________________ Date ____________

Goal!

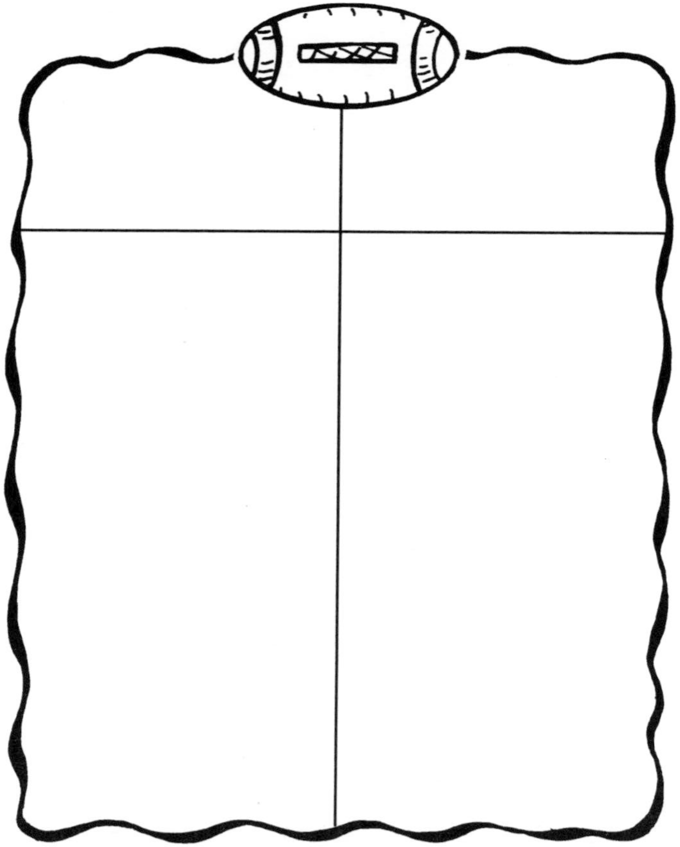

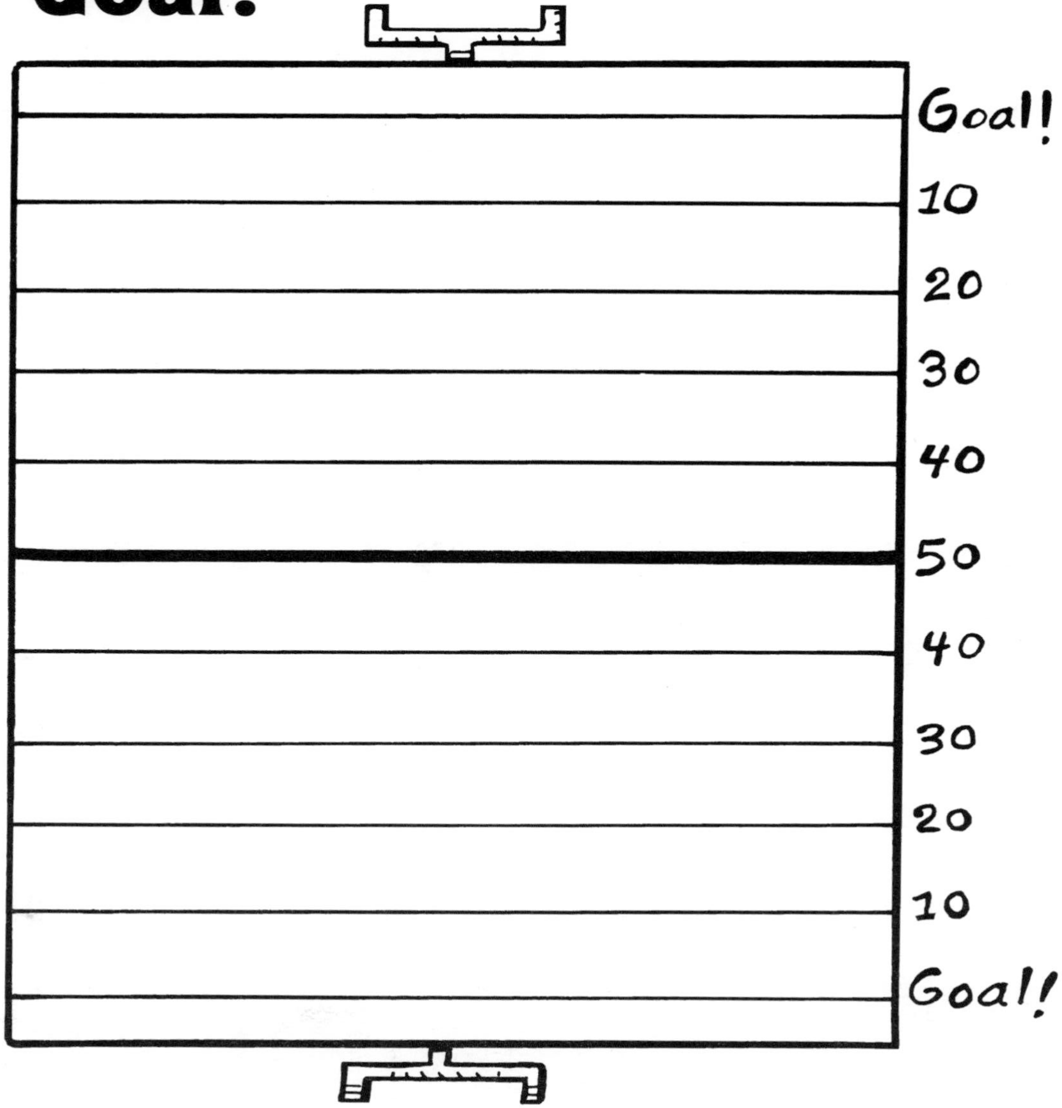
Goal!
10
20
30
40
50
40
30
20
10
Goal!

Skill

- Forming Contractions
- Analyzing Spelling Changes

Management Tip

Use this organizer to model how to form and spell specific kinds of contractions, such as *will* contractions *(we'll, he'll, she'll)*. Later, students can use it to form a variety of contractions.

Literature Link

If You're Not Here, Please Raise Your Hand: Poems About School by Kalli Dakos (Aladdin, 1995).

This delightful collection of poems covers a variety of humorous and sensitive school experiences.

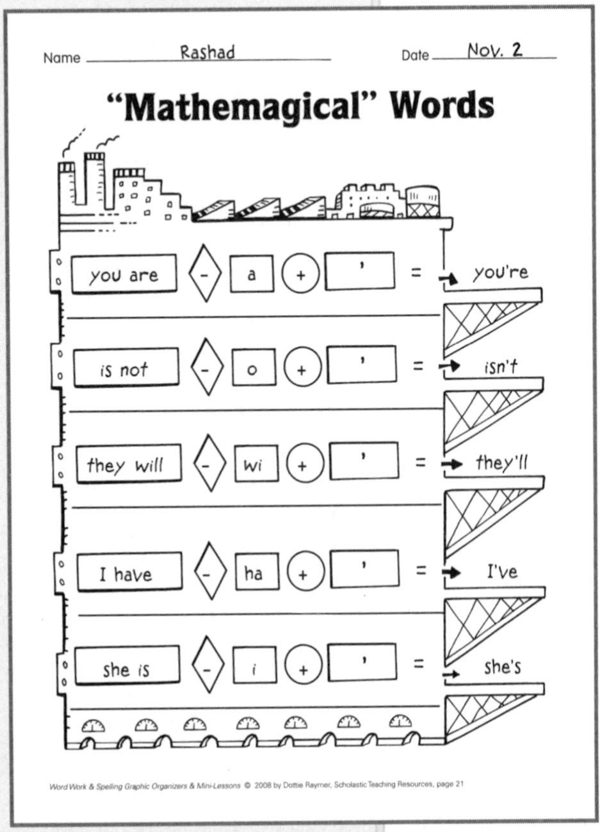
Name Rashad Date Nov. 2

"Mathemagical" Words

you are	-	a	+	'	=	you're
is not	-	o	+	'	=	isn't
they will	-	wi	+	'	=	they'll
I have	-	ha	+	'	=	I've
she is	-	i	+	'	=	she's

Word Work & Spelling Graphic Organizers & Mini-Lessons © 2008 by Dottie Raymer, Scholastic Teaching Resources, page 21

"Mathemagical" Words

Purpose

Students track the spelling changes that occur when forming contractions.

Introducing the Activity

Explain to students that making contractions is much like solving an equation. Write *did* and *not* on the board. Ask: *How can these two words be made into one word?* Lead students to understand that one letter must be taken away and an apostrophe added to make the contraction *didn't*. Write an equation to represent the process:

did not − o + ' = didn't

Using the Graphic Organizer

1. Display five word pairs that can be used to form a particular kind of contraction, such as *not* contractions (*is not, have not, would not, are not,* and *did not).*
2. Distribute copies of the graphic organizer. Have students write a word pair in the first shape in the first equation. Ask: *How can this word pair be turned into one word?* After students respond, show them how to place a minus sign (–) in the second shape and the letter (or letters) to be subtracted in the next shape.
3. Explain: *When letters are removed to make a contraction, an apostrophe is added to indicate that letters are missing.* Have students write a plus sign (+) and an apostrophe (') in the next two shapes.
4. To balance the equation, have them write the final contraction in the shape to the right of the equal sign (=).
5. Instruct students to "balance" equations for the other word pairs, writing the math signs, letters, and apostrophes in the appropriate shapes.

Taking It Further

Have students use this organizer to explore how the spelling of a word changes when an ending is added, such as a plural ending (*bunny/bunnies, wolf/wolves*), verb ending (*fly/flies, run/running, make/making*), or suffix (*happy/happily/happiness, explode/explosion*).

Name ______________________________ Date ______________

"Mathemagical" Words

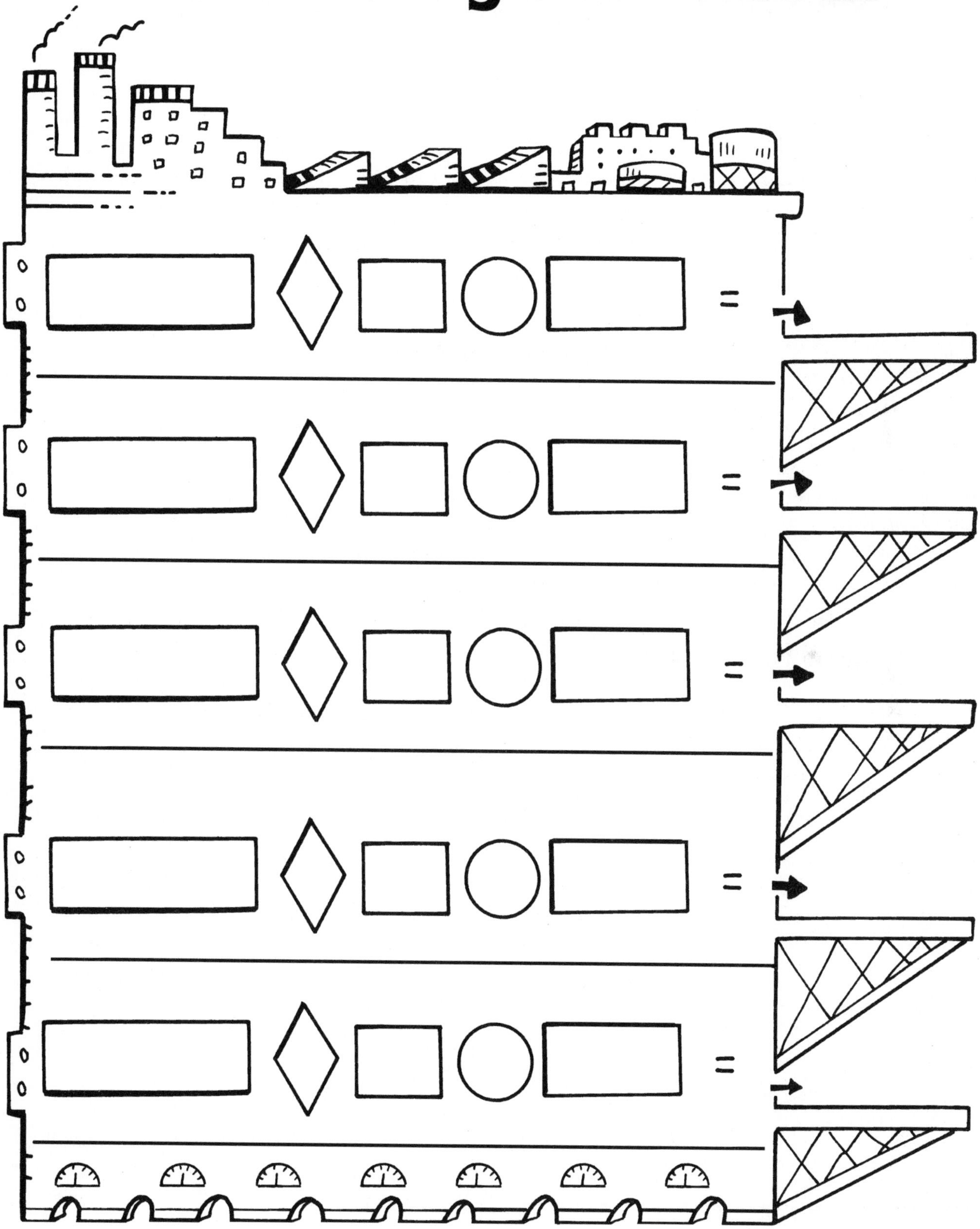

Skill

- Recognizing Syllables in Words
- Dividing Words Into Syllables
- Identifying Accented Syllables in Words

Management Tip

Model how to use this organizer on the overhead projector. Keep a dictionary on hand for students to refer to as they complete the organizer.

Literature Link

Destination Mars by Seymour Simon (HarperTrophy, 2004).

Fascinating facts and actual photos highlight this book about our solar system's red planet.

Syllable Caterpillar

Purpose

Students use their knowledge of spelling patterns and word structure to divide words into syllables.

Introducing the Activity

Tell students that writers often find it useful to divide words into recognizable chunks when spelling multi-syllable words. List several two-, three-, and four-syllable words. Then work with students to divide each word into syllables, reminding them that each syllable contains only one vowel sound. Point out any common syllable patterns that emerge as well as the accented syllable in each word.

Using the Graphic Organizer

1. Select a multi-syllable word that contains a common syllable pattern, such as *destination*. Write the word on the first leaf on the graphic organizer. Then say the word aloud slowly, breaking it into syllables.
2. Ask students to identify the first syllable in the word and its vowel sound. Frame that syllable with your fingers. Then write it on the first section of the caterpillar to the right of the leaf.
3. Repeat to identify the remaining syllables in the word. Then say the word again, this time having students listen for the syllable that is emphasized, or accented. You might lightly color the section of the caterpillar containing the accented syllable.
4. In the second and third leaves, write other words that share the same syllable pattern as the first word, such as *fascination* and *separation*. Repeat steps 2 and 3 for each word. Then discuss with students the syllable patterns they detect in the words on the caterpillars.
5. Distribute copies of the organizer for students to complete using another set of words that share a common syllable pattern.

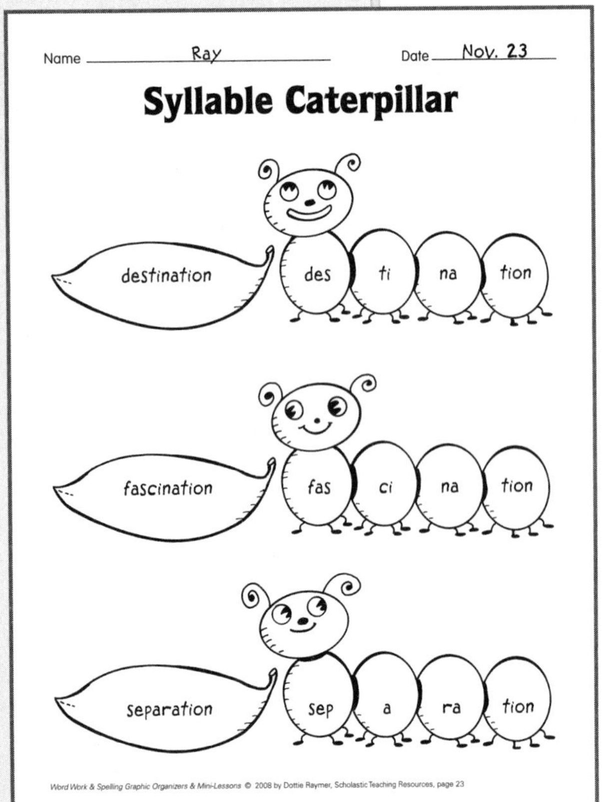
Name Ray
Date Nov. 23
Syllable Caterpillar
destination
des
ti
na
tion
fascination
fas
ci
na
tion
separation
sep
a
ra
tion
Word Work & Spelling Graphic Organizers & Mini-Lessons © 2008 by Dottie Raymer, Scholastic Teaching Resources, page 23

Taking It Further

Use the organizer to encourage students to examine syllables in words they encounter every day, such as their names, the school's name, classroom furniture, book titles, and so on.

Name ______________________________ Date ________________

Syllable Caterpillar

Skill

- Recognizing Compound Words
- Identifying Words in Compound Words
- Forming Compound Words

Management Tip

After students are familiar with how to use this organizer, use it as a time-filler activity to reinforce vocabulary skills.

Literature Link

Everything on a Waffle by Polly Horvath (Farrar, Straus and Giroux, 2004).

After her parents are lost at sea, Primrose goes to live with her Uncle Jack where she encounters misadventures, misunderstandings, and a very special friend.

Compound Word Puzzle

Purpose

Students explore how words are combined to create compound words.

Introducing the Activity

Explain that compound words are made up of two or more smaller words that have been combined to create a new word. Ask students to brainstorm compound words, such as *cupcake, horseshoe,* and *suitcase.* Write their responses on the board. Then ask them to identify each smaller word contained in the compound words. Invite volunteers to draw a line between the combined words.

Using the Graphic Organizer

1. Choose several two-part compound words in which some of the smaller words can be interchanged to create other compound words, such as *someone, anybody, everything,* and *daytime.* Write the words on the board.
2. Distribute copies of the graphic organizer to students. Have them write each compound word on a pair of puzzle pieces, recording the first word from the combination on the left piece and the second word on the right piece.
3. Invite a volunteer to choose two words from the puzzles that can be combined to create a compound word not already used. Have students write that word on a line at the bottom of the page. Then challenge students to create as many other compound words as possible to write on the lines. Afterward, invite them to share their words with the class.
4. Distribute new copies of the organizer for students to complete using compound words of their own choice.

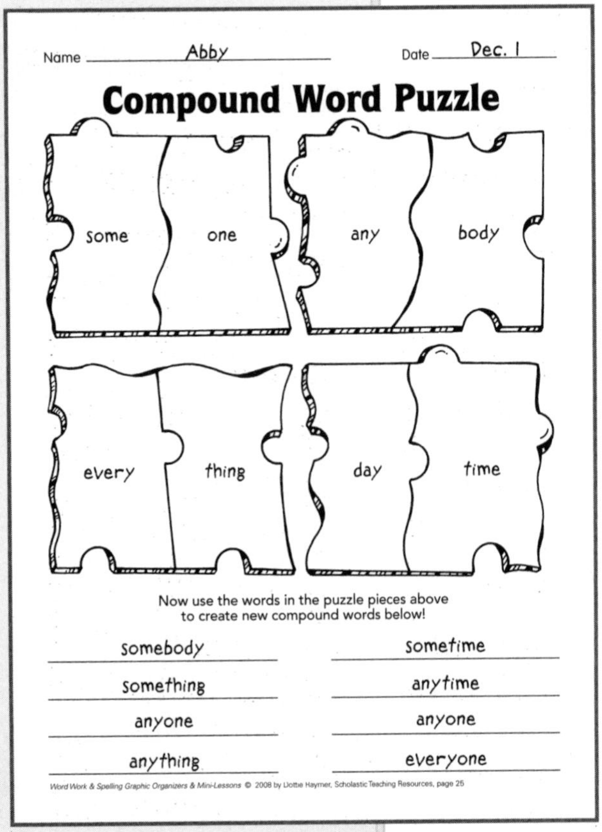
Name Abby Date Dec. 1

Compound Word Puzzle

some | one | any | body
every | thing | day | time

Now use the words in the puzzle pieces above to create new compound words below!

somebody | sometime
something | anytime
anyone | anyone
anything | everyone

Word Work & Spelling Graphic Organizers & Mini-Lessons © 2008 by Liottie Haymer, Scholastic Teaching Resources, page 25

Taking It Further

Have pairs or small groups of students challenge each other to see how many new compound words they can make from the same set of compound words.

Name ______________________________ Date ______________

Compound Word Puzzle

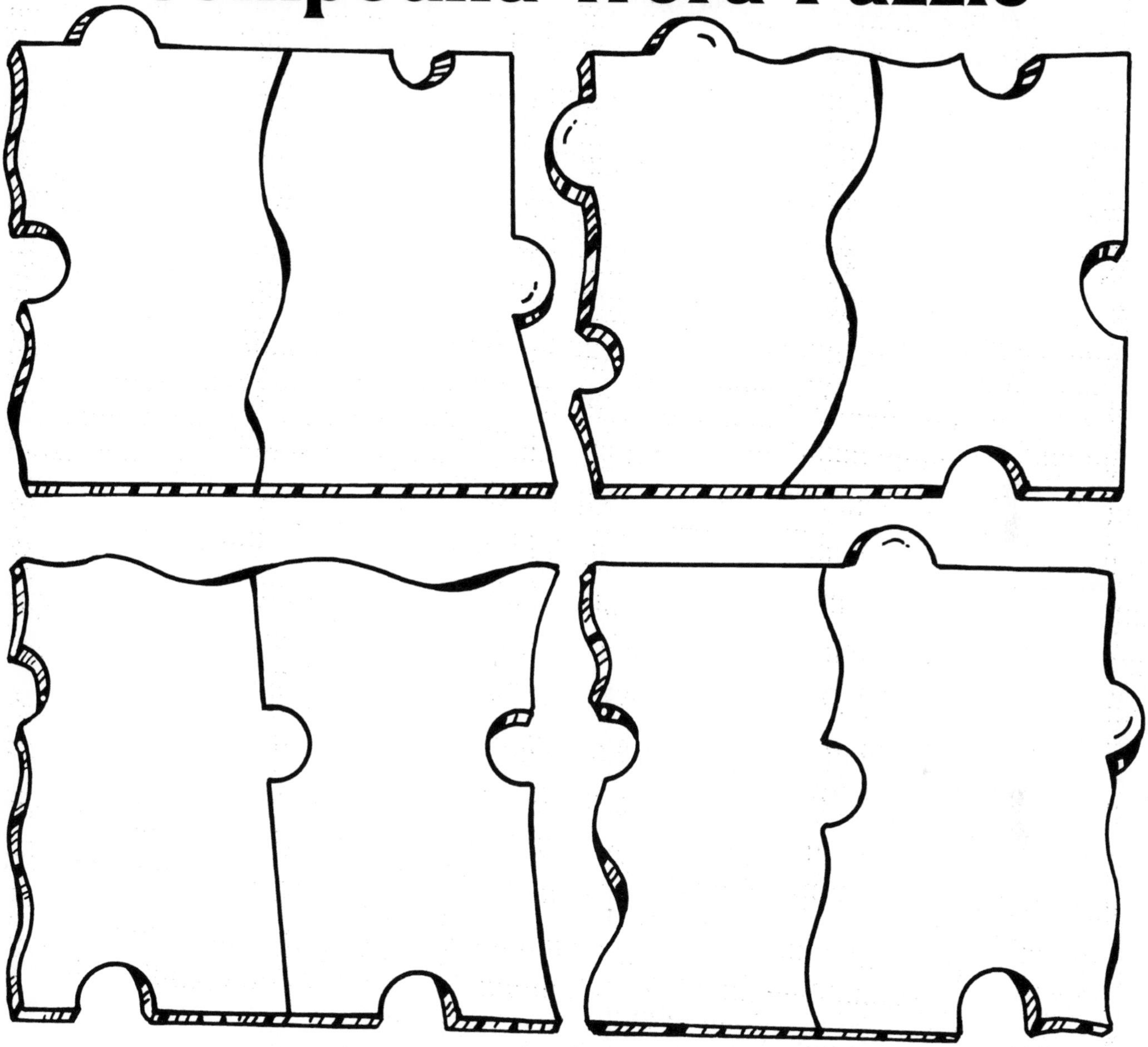

Now use the words in the puzzle pieces above to create new compound words below!

______________________ ______________________

______________________ ______________________

______________________ ______________________

______________________ ______________________

Skill

- Differentiating Homophones and Easily-Confused Words
- Using Spelling Recall Strategies

Management Tip

Model the use of this organizer on the overhead projector. Then encourage students to complete it independently or in pairs.

Literature Link

A Chocolate Moose for Dinner by Fred Gwynne (Aladdin, 2005).

In this clever book about confusing words, a little girl has her own interpretation of the words and phrases used by her parents.

Homophone Clues

Purpose

Students create strategies to help them recall the correct spelling of homophone pairs and words that are easily confused.

Introducing the Activity

Write *hair* and *hare* on the board. Explain that these words are homophones—words that sound the same but have different spellings and meanings. Ask students to tell what each word means. Then write *desert* and *dessert.* Point out that these two nouns are often confused with each other. Then have students define each one (*desert* is a dry, barren land; *dessert* is a sweet food). Afterward, tell them that they will use this organizer to create strategies to help them remember how to spell homophones and easily confused words.

Using the Graphic Organizer

1. Choose two homophones or easily confused words. Write one word in the "Word" section of the top truck on the graphic organizer. Write the other word on the bottom truck.
2. Make up a sentence for each word, trying to include a mnemonic or other device that will aid in recalling the word's spelling. Write each sentence in the appropriate section on the truck.
3. Using a "think-aloud" method, model how you came up with the mnemonic or strategy. For example, you might say: *The word* dessert *has two s's. Both of the words in* super sweet *start with* s. *So whenever I want to remember how to spell* dessert, *I think about super sweet!* Write a brief description of your strategy in the "Clue" section for each word.
4. Draw a picture in the "Picture" section that represents the spelling and meaning of the word.
5. Distribute copies of the organizer for students to complete with a pair of homophones or easily confused words. When finished, invite them to share their strategies with the class.

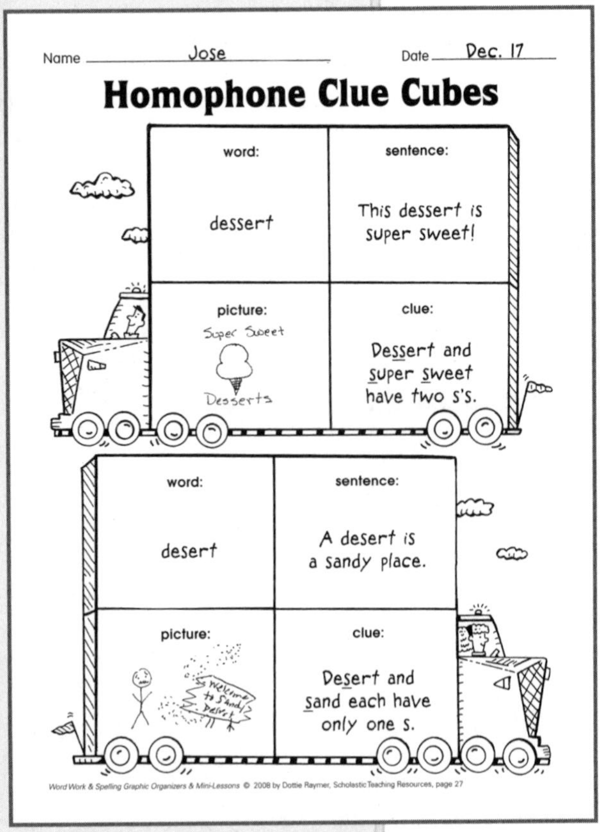

Name Jose
Date Dec. 17
Homophone Clue Cubes
word:
dessert
sentence:
This dessert is super sweet!
picture:
Super Sweet
Desserts
clue:
Dessert and super sweet have two s's.
word:
desert
sentence:
A desert is a sandy place.
picture:
clue:
Desert and sand each have only one s.
Word Work & Spelling Graphic Organizers & Mini-Lessons © 2008 by Dottie Raymer, Scholastic Teaching Resources, page 27

Taking It Further

Invite students to develop strategies to help them recall weekly spelling words. Encourage them to share and discuss their methods with the class.

Name ______________________ Date ____________

Homophone Clue Cubes

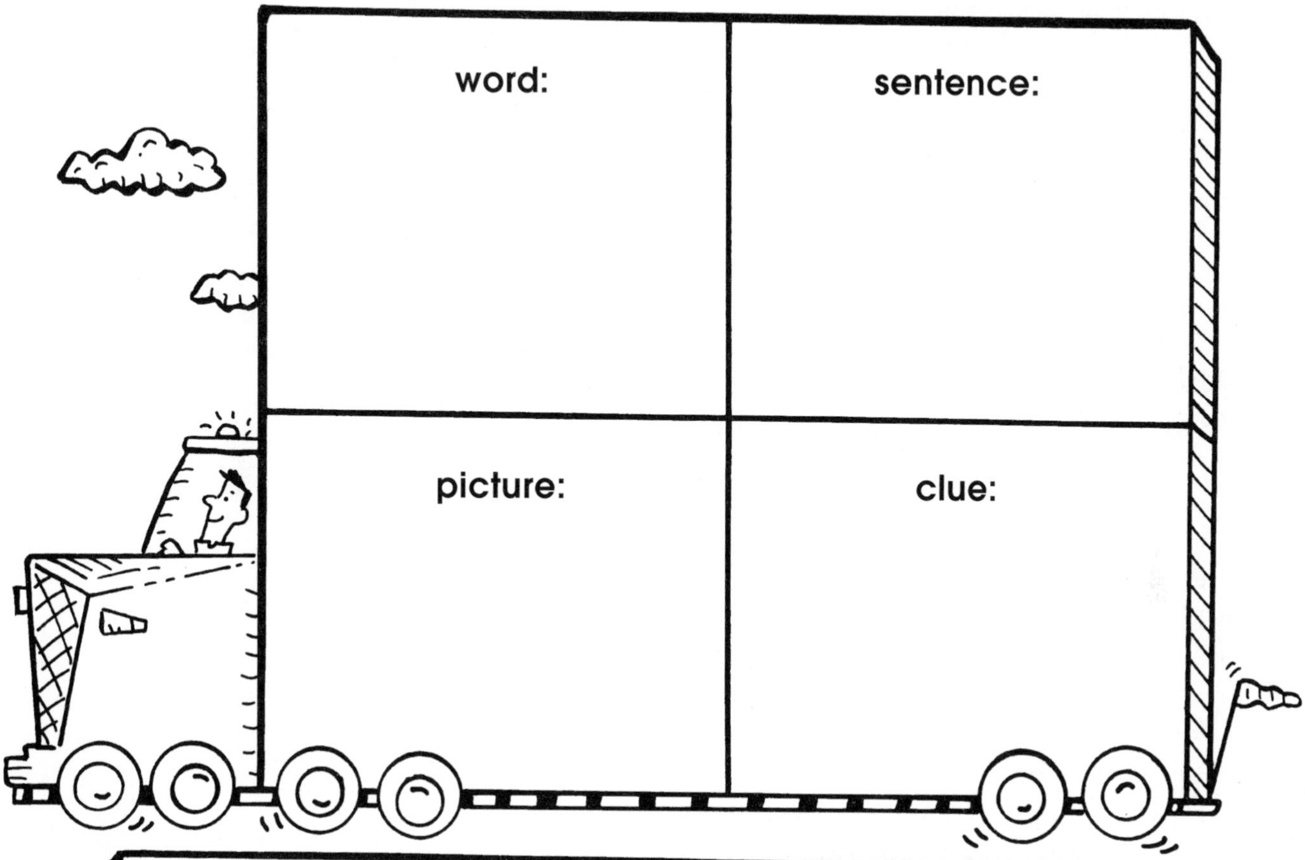
word:
sentence:
picture:
clue:

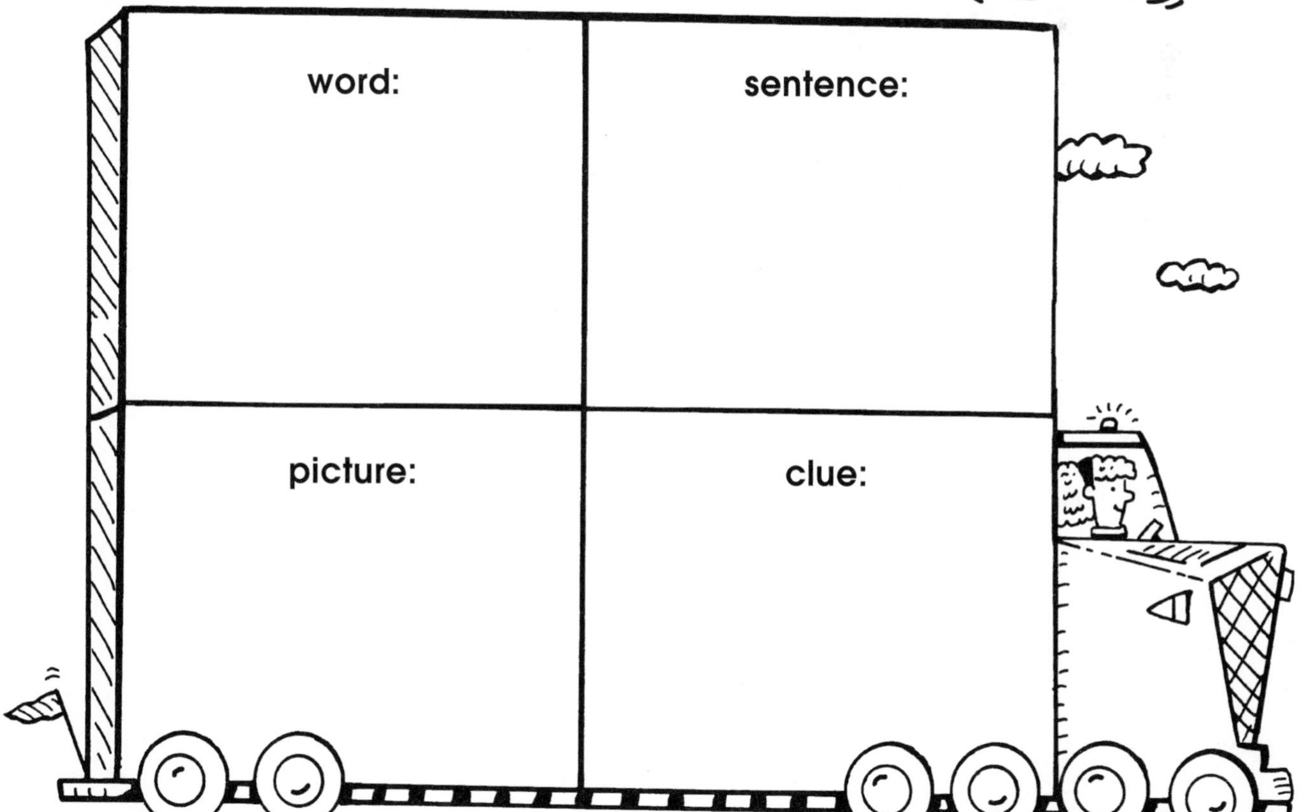
word:
sentence:
picture:
clue:

Skyscraper Spelling

Skill

- Using Spelling Strategies
- Reinforcing Visual and Auditory Memory

Management Tip

After modeling how to complete this organizer, use it with students when introducing new spelling words.

Literature Link

Amelia Bedelia 4 Mayor
by Herman Parish (HarperTrophy, 2001).

When Amelia's boss expresses discontent with the mayor and says she should run for the office, that's just what Amelia does!

Purpose

Students spell new words using a look-and-say strategy.

Introducing the Activity

Tell students that different learners rely on different methods to remember how to spell words. One student might recall the sounds heard in a word while saying it aloud, another might form a mental picture of the word, while another might write the word several times to help remember its spelling and shape. Explain that with this graphic organizer, they will use a look-and-say strategy to help improve their success in spelling.

Using the Graphic Organizer

1. Distribute copies of the graphic organizer. Write a spelling word on the board and have students copy it in the first box under "Look and Say."
2. Say the word aloud slowly, tracking the letters with your finger. Point out any difficult letters or word parts. Repeat several times, having students join you by saying and tracking the word on their organizers.
3. Cover the word. Have students also cover the word on their pages. Then ask them to write the word under "Cover and Spell." Encourage them to say the word to themselves, listening for the letter sounds and trying to visualize its spelling.
4. Instruct students to uncover the word in the first column and compare their spelling to it. Have them mark the "Look and Check" box to indicate whether or not they spelled the word correctly. If incorrect, have them discuss their errors and suggest strategies that might help them spell the word correctly. Then have them write the word correctly under "Make It Correct."
5. Repeat steps 2–4 for each spelling word you introduce to students. To begin, you might use words that follow a specific spelling pattern or rule. Later, students can use the organizer to practice spelling a variety of words.

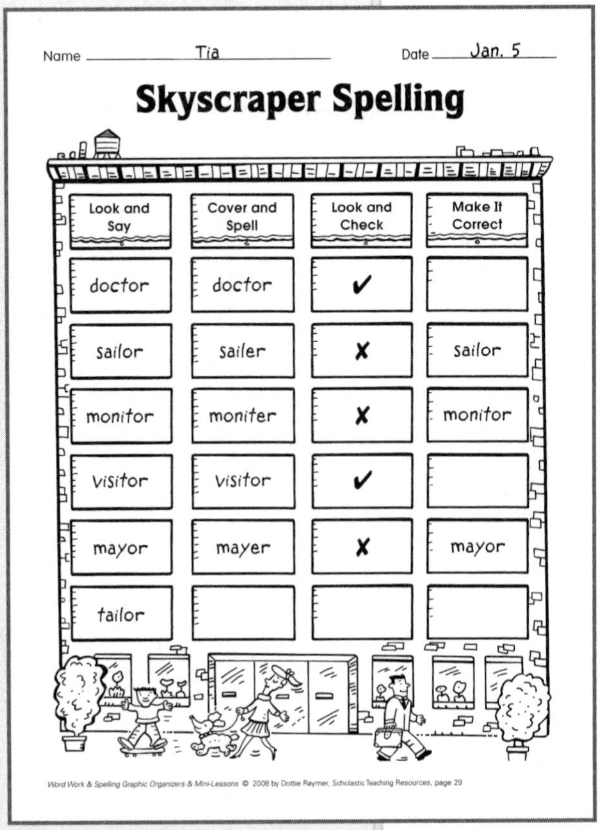

Name Tia Date Jan. 5

Skyscraper Spelling

Look and Say	Cover and Spell	Look and Check	Make It Correct
doctor	doctor	✓	
sailor	sailer	✗	sailor
monitor	moniter	✗	monitor
visitor	visitor	✓	
mayor	mayer	✗	mayor
tailor			

Taking It Further

Have students use the organizer to learn how to spell words related to a topic of study, such as plant-related words.

Name ______________________________ Date ________________

Skyscraper Spelling

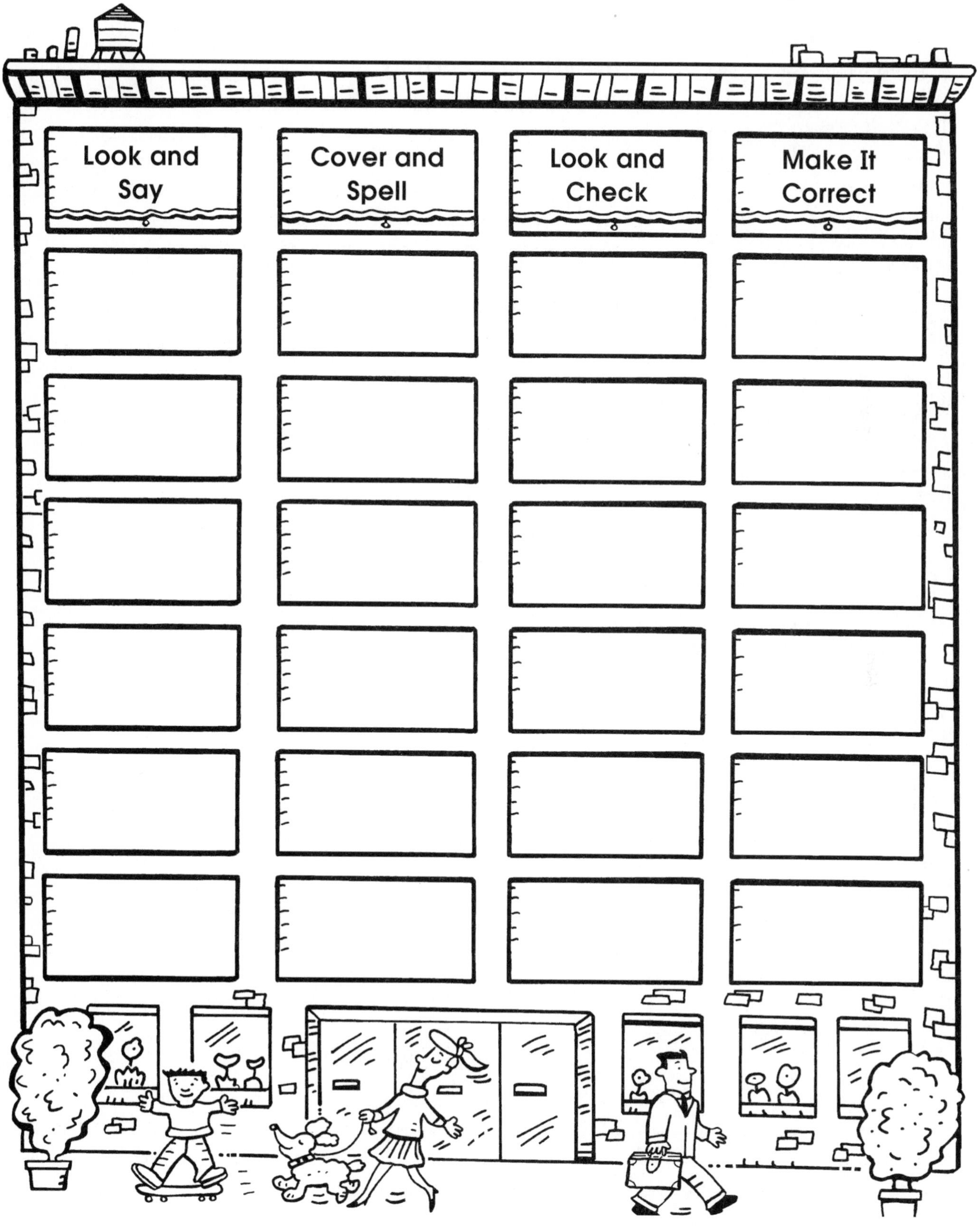
Look and Say
Cover and Spell
Look and Check
Make It Correct

Spelling Survey Says...!

Skill

- Grouping Words by Spelling Patterns
- Recognizing Words in Different Contexts
- Making Spelling Generalizations

Management Tip

Model how to use this organizer with small reading groups, using texts that students are working with at the time.

Literature Link

The Midnight Fox by Betsy Byars (Puffin, 1981).

Tom expects to have a miserable summer at his aunt's farm—until he discovers a fox and its secret.

Purpose

Students examine and group words by spelling patterns.

Introducing the Activity

Tell students that they will encounter many words in their reading that follow the same or similar spelling patterns. To demonstrate, read aloud a passage, pausing to list each plural word from the text on the board. When finished, invite students to help you group the words by their plural spelling patterns. Then explain that most plurals follow specific spelling rules. Review the rule represented by each word group.

Using the Graphic Organizer

1. Choose a general word structure concept that students are familiar with—such as plural nouns—and that applies to several categories of words (for example, pluralizing words that end in double *s*, *x*, and any other consonant).
2. Write a brief description of each category in a column at the top of the graph on the graphic organizer. Then have students search their text to find words belonging to each category. Write their findings in the appropriate columns, starting at the bottom and working up.
3. After a given period of time, have students examine the words on the graph. Ask: *Do the words in each column follow a pattern?* Invite students to share their observations. For example, they might respond that to make words ending in double *s* and *x* plural, an *es* is added to the end of the word, but for words that end in other consonants, only an *s* is added.
4. Have students share what they notice about the results of their graphs. Ask: *Does one pattern occur more often than another? Why?*
5. Distribute copies of the organizer for students to complete using other categories of spelling patterns (such as adding *er* to words that end in a single consonant, double consonant, and *y*).

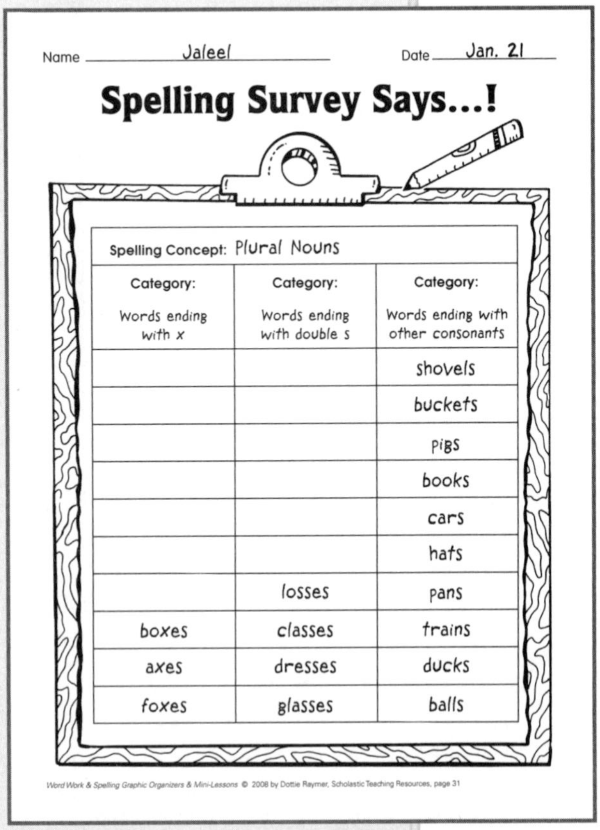

Name Jaleel Date Jan. 21

Spelling Survey Says...!

Spelling Concept: Plural Nouns

Category: Words ending with x	Category: Words ending with double s	Category: Words ending with other consonants
		shovels
		buckets
		pigs
		books
		cars
		hats
	losses	pans
boxes	classes	trains
axes	dresses	ducks
foxes	glasses	balls

Taking It Further

Have students group words by various spelling rules, such as those that apply to contractions, vowel pairs, and letter combinations that represent multiple sounds (as in *how* and *row*)

Name ______________________________ Date ________________

Spelling Survey Says...!

Spelling Concept:		
Category:	Category:	Category:

Special Spelling Secret

Skill

- Recognizing Spelling Patterns
- Identifying Spelling Rules

Management Tip

Have students fill out a copy of this organizer while you model how to complete it on the overhead projector. Later, they can work in pairs to determine the spelling secret of other sets of words.

Literature Link

The Errant Knight by Ann Tompert (Illumination Arts Publishing Company, 2003).

On the way to answer the call from his king, a loyal, but compassionate, knight makes frequent stops to help others in need.

Purpose

Students examine words that contain a common spelling pattern to discover the spelling "secret."

Introducing the Activity

Write *funniest, silliest, happiest,* and *bumpiest* on the board. Ask students to examine the words to try to discover what they all have in common. Invite them to share their observations. After determining that the words all end with *iest,* challenge students to formulate a rule that applies to the spelling pattern (in this case, "when a word ends in a consonant + *y,* change the *y* to *i* before adding *est*"). Invite them to brainstorm other words that follow the pattern (*heaviest, earliest, sleepiest,* and so on).

Using the Graphic Organizer

1. Distribute copies of the graphic organizer. Write four words on the board that follow a specific spelling rule or pattern (such as *knob, knife, knight,* and *knit*). Write each word on a clam and have students do the same.
2. Ask students to examine the words to try to find a common spelling pattern or rule that applies to all of them. Instruct them to raise their hand once they think they know the spelling secret. Invite volunteers to share their discoveries, discussing each different response as a class and checking to see if the rule is valid for all the words.
3. Model how to write the spelling secret on the ink cloud to the left of the octopus. Have students do the same.
4. Ask students to write other words that follow the rule on the ink cloud to the right of the octopus. Discuss and compare their responses.

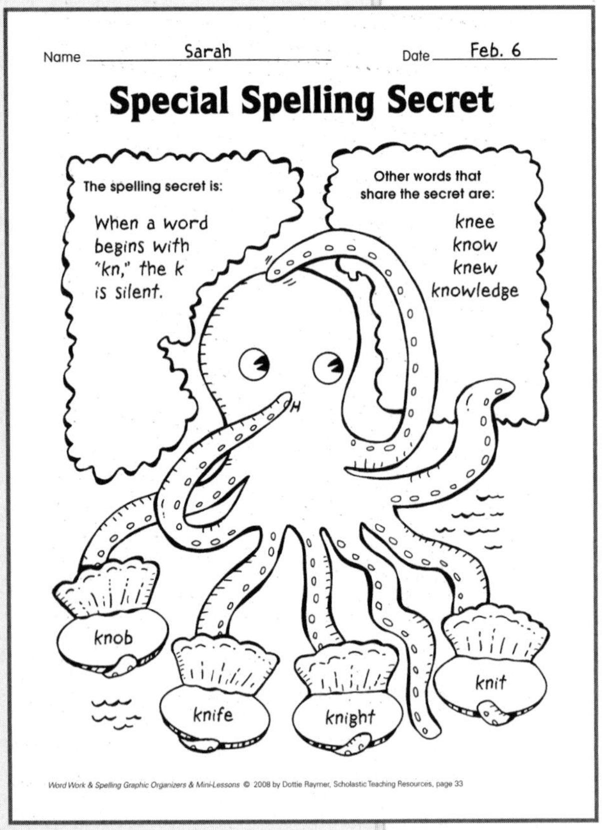

Name Sarah
Date Feb. 6
Special Spelling Secret
The spelling secret is:
When a word begins with "kn," the k is silent.
Other words that share the secret are:
knee
know
knew
knowledge
knob
knife
knight
knit
Word Work & Spelling Graphic Organizers & Mini-Lessons © 2008 by Dottie Raymer, Scholastic Teaching Resources, page 33

Taking It Further

Challenge students to write words on the clams to represent a spelling secret that they have determined on their own. Have them exchange organizers with others to see if classmates can discover the secret that applies to their words.

Name ______________________ Date ______________

Special Spelling Secret

The spelling secret is:
Other words that share the secret are:

Skill

- Creating Mnemonics for Difficult Words
- Identifying Exceptions to Common Spelling Rules

Management Tip

Model how to use this organizer on the overhead projector. Then have students complete it on their own or in pairs.

Literature Link

Frog and Toad Are Friends by Arnold Lobel (HarperTrophy, 2003).

Frog and Toad enjoy each other's friendship during many kinds of adventures.

Outlaw Words

Purpose

Students create mnemonic devices to help them recall how to spell words with tricky spellings.

Introducing the Activity

Share a familiar mnemonic device that people use to help remember a word's spelling, such as "The principal is my pal at school, and the principle I follow is a rule." Explain that strategies that help people remember things are called *mnemonics*. Invite students to share other mnemonics they know that apply to spelling words. Afterward, tell them that mnemonic devices are especially helpful strategies to use when trying to remember how to spell "outlaw" words—words that have tricky spellings.

Using the Graphic Organizer

1. Choose two "outlaw" words that students often have difficulty spelling. You might consider words with tricky spellings, such as those that contain silent letters *(scissors, rhythm)*, are easily confused *(council, counsel)*, or are exceptions to general spelling rules *(weird, seize)*, or words that include double letters *(accommodate, occurrence)*, suffixes *(remarkable, possible)*, or unusual letter combinations *(foreign, vacuum)*. Write each outlaw word on a poster on the graphic organizer.
2. Examine the first word with students. Discuss why they might have difficulty spelling the word. If desired, circle the part that might give them trouble. For example, you might circle *ie* in *friend.*
3. Have students make up mnemonics to help them remember the word's spelling. After sharing, choose one to write at the bottom of the poster as the "Capture Clue."
4. Repeat steps 2 and 3 for the other word.
5. Distribute copies of the organizer for students to use with other outlaw words.

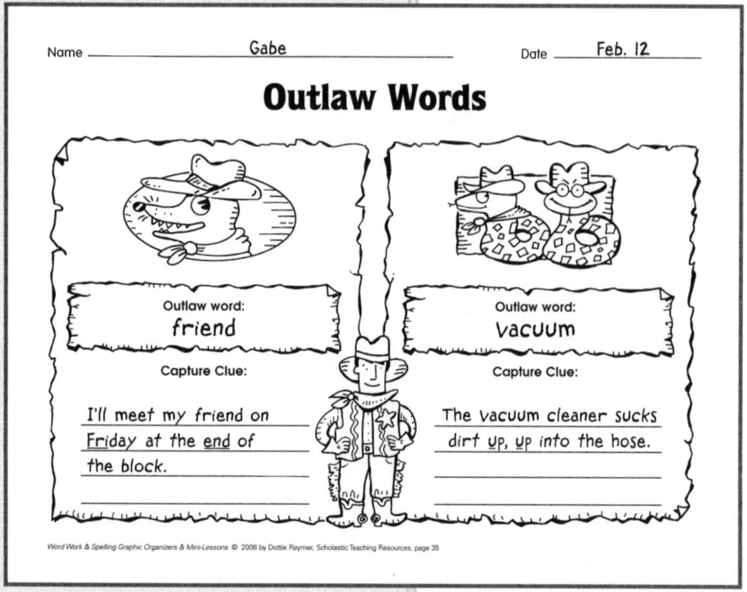

Name Gabe Date Feb. 12

Outlaw Words

Outlaw word: friend

Capture Clue: I'll meet my friend on Friday at the end of the block.

Outlaw word: vacuum

Capture Clue: The vacuum cleaner sucks dirt up, up into the hose.

Word Work & Spelling Graphic Organizers & Mini-Lessons © 2008 by Dottie Raymer, Scholastic Teaching Resources, page 35

Taking It Further

Compile the completed posters into a class booklet for students to refer to whenever they encounter outlaw words in their writing activities.

Name ______________________ Date ______________

Outlaw Words

Outlaw word:

Capture Clue:

____

____

____

____

Outlaw word:

Capture Clue:

____

____

____

____

Seeing Suffixes

Skill

- Adding Suffixes
- Identifying Spelling Patterns of Suffixes
- Inferring Spelling Generalizations

Management Tip

Model how to use this organizer on the overhead projector. Then have pairs or small groups complete it for other suffixes.

Literature Link

The Stories Julian Tells by Ann Cameron (Dell Yearling, 2001).

Julian's imaginative stories lead him into mischief, but also help him learn valuable life lessons.

Purpose

Students explore the spelling rules used when adding suffixes to words.

Introducing the Activity

Explain that when certain suffixes are added to a root word, one or more letters in the root may be added, dropped, or exchanged for another letter. For example, when adding *ing* to *place,* the silent *e* is dropped *(placing)* while *clap* gains a consonant *(clapping)* in the process. Tell students that they will add suffixes to words to explore how these endings affect spelling.

Using the Graphic Organizer

1. Explain that after completing the graphic organizer, students will see words in the crystal ball that follow a similar spelling pattern whenever a suffix is added.
2. Choose a spelling rule that applies to adding suffixes, such as "change the *y* to *i* before adding *es* to a word that ends in a consonant + *y*." Write a few words that follow the rule—such as *flies* and *stories*—in the crystal ball.
3. Around the outside of the ball, write several words containing the same suffix form but that do not follow the rule (for example, *boys* and *keys*).
4. Have students examine the words in and around the ball. Ask: *Do you see a spelling pattern in the suffix endings of the words in the ball?* If needed, add other words to provide more examples. As students detect the pattern, have them share their observations and name words to add to the organizer. Guide them to state the spelling rule that applies to the words in the ball. Write the rule on the cloth.
5. Distribute copies of the organizer. Provide another set of words with suffixes for students to use to complete the organizer.

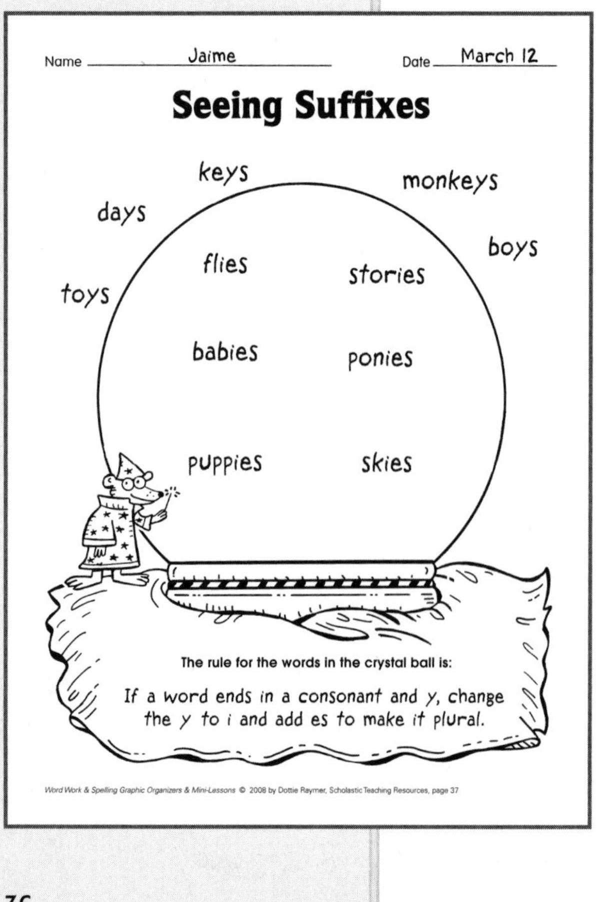
Name Jaime
Date March 12
Seeing Suffixes
keys
monkeys
days
boys
toys
flies
stories
babies
ponies
puppies
skies
The rule for the words in the crystal ball is:
If a word ends in a consonant and y, change the y to i and add es to make it plural.
Word Work & Spelling Graphic Organizers & Mini-Lessons © 2008 by Dottie Raymer, Scholastic Teaching Resources, page 37

Taking It Further

Invite pairs to label paper crystal balls with spelling rules for adding suffixes, such as dropping a silent *e* or doubling a consonant when adding *ing*. Display these "reminders" in the writing center.

Name ______________________________ Date ______________

Seeing Suffixes

The rule for the words in the crystal ball is:

Skill

- Adding Affixes to Root Words
- Identifying Root Words
- Exploring Meanings of Words With Affixes

Management Tip

After demonstrating how to use this organizer, use it with students to help build new vocabulary and reinforce understanding of word structure.

Literature Link

Working Cotton by Sherley Anne Williams (Voyager Books, 1997).

Shelan describes a day in the difficult life of her migrant family as they work in the cotton fields.

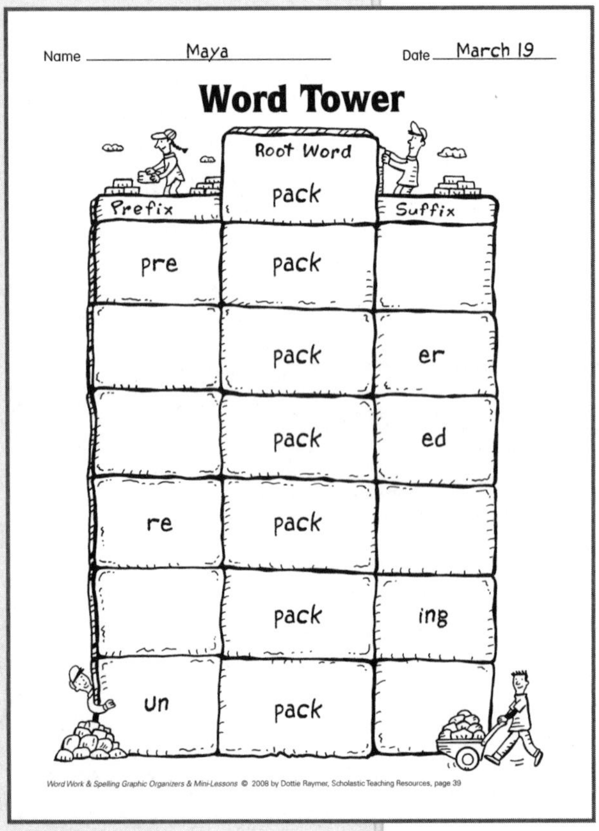

Name Maya
Date March 19
Word Tower
Root Word
Prefix
Suffix
pack
pre
pack
pack
er
pack
ed
re
pack
pack
ing
un
pack
Word Work & Spelling Graphic Organizers & Mini-Lessons © 2008 by Dottie Raymer, Scholastic Teaching Resources, page 39

Word Tower

Purpose

Students explore how adding prefixes or suffixes to a root word changes its meaning and sometimes spelling.

Introducing the Activity

Write *refold, folding, folded, unfold,* and *folder* on the board. Ask: *What do these words have in common?* Lead students to discover that they all share the same root word, *fold.* Then invite volunteers to point out each prefix or suffix that has been added to *fold.* Discuss whether or not the affix changed the spelling of the root word and how the meaning of the new word differs from the original.

Using the Graphic Organizer

1. Choose a root word to which several prefixes and suffixes can be attached without changing its spelling (for example, *pack, work,* or *play*). Distribute copies of the graphic organizer and have students write this word in each block in the center column of the tower.
2. Ask them to write a prefix, such as *pre,* in the first row under "Prefix." Ask: *What word is created when this prefix is added to the root word?* Invite a volunteer to respond and tell what the new word means.
3. Repeat step 2, this time using *er* in the next row under "Suffix."
4. Have students fill in a different prefix or suffix on each row of the tower. Then invite them to read the words that can be created by attaching each affix to the root word. Encourage them to tell how the meaning of each new word differs from the root word.
5. Have students use the organizer to explore attaching affixes to a variety of root words. Discuss how the spelling of the root word changes in some instances, such as when the final *y* in *happy* is changed to *i* to create *happily.*

Taking It Further

Challenge students to use the organizer to create words that contain both a prefix and suffix, such as *unhappily, overacting, illegally,* and *unemployment.*

Name ______________________________ Date ________________

Word Tower

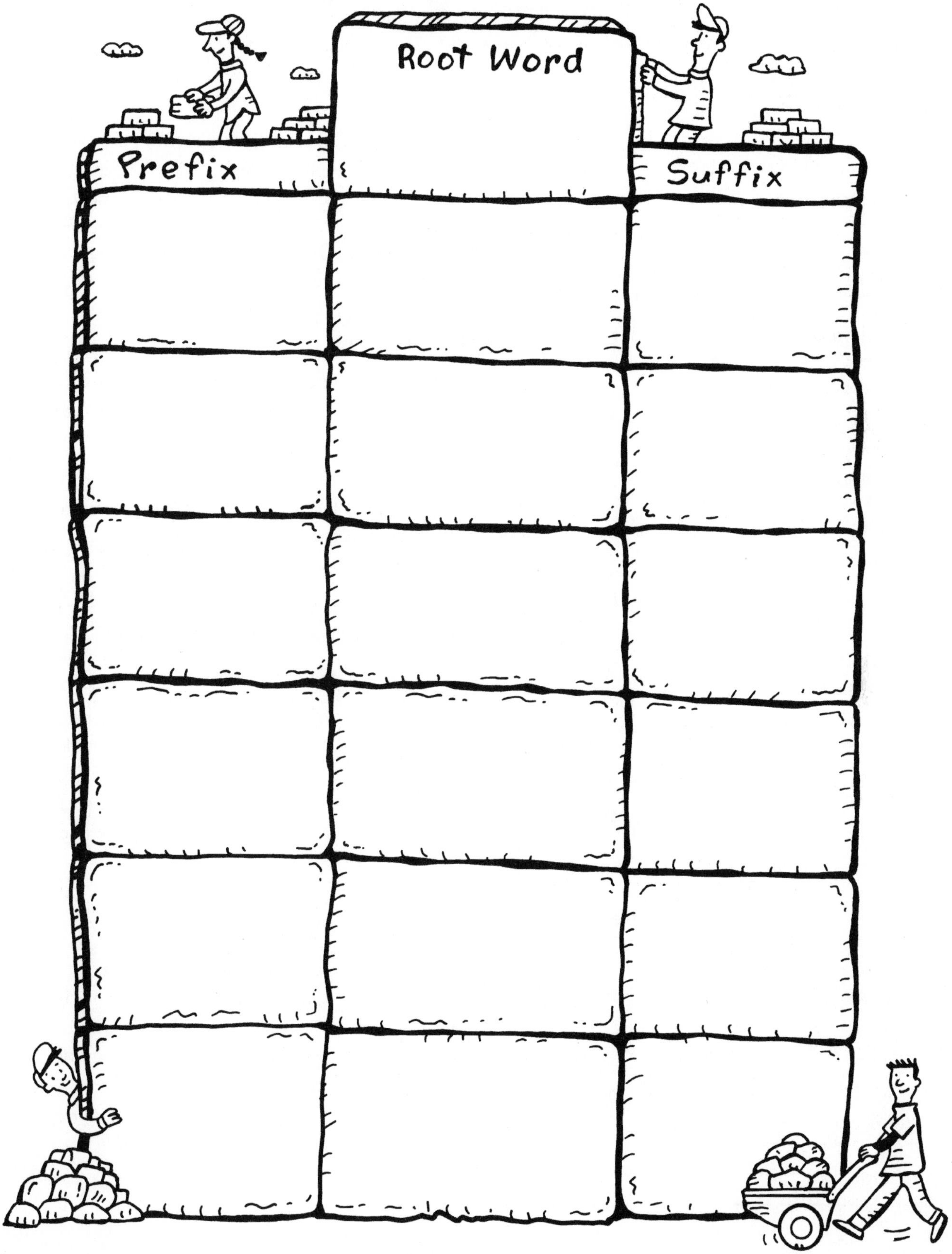
Root Word
Prefix
Suffix

Skill

- Identifying Prefixes, Suffixes, and Root Words
- Creating New Words

Management Tip

After students are familiar with how to use this organizer, invite pairs to complete it, with each partner choosing a bicycle wheel to fill in.

Literature Link

Uncommon Traveler: Mary Kingsley in Africa by Don Brown (Houghton Mifflin, 2003).

After an unhappy childhood spent caring for her mother, 30-year-old Mary does the unthinkable for proper ladies of her time—she travels alone to West Africa.

Word Part Bicycle

Purpose

Students apply what they know about spelling, word meaning, and common prefixes, suffixes, and roots to broaden their vocabularies.

Introducing the Activity

Review the meaning of a prefix, suffix, and root word. Then list a few words that contain a root word and prefix or suffix, such as *reread, mistreat, untie, loudly, careful,* and *leader*. For each word, ask students to identify the root word and its prefix or suffix. Talk about how the affix altered the word's meaning. Then invite students to brainstorm other words that contain prefixes or suffixes.

Using the Graphic Organizer

1. Write a prefix in the middle of the left bicycle wheel on the graphic organizer. Choose a prefix that frequently appears in students' reading materials, such as *un.*
2. Ask students to name words that contain that prefix. They might respond with words such as *unhappy, undone,* and *unknown.* Record each word on a different section of the wheel.
3. After filling in all the sections on the wheel, have students identify the root word and prefix in each word. Invite volunteers to tell how the prefix changes the meaning of the root word.
4. Write a different prefix in the right wheel. Then repeat steps 2 and 3.
5. Distribute copies of the organizer. Provide two suffixes for students to enter on the bicycle wheels. Have them complete the organizer and then discuss their responses with the class.

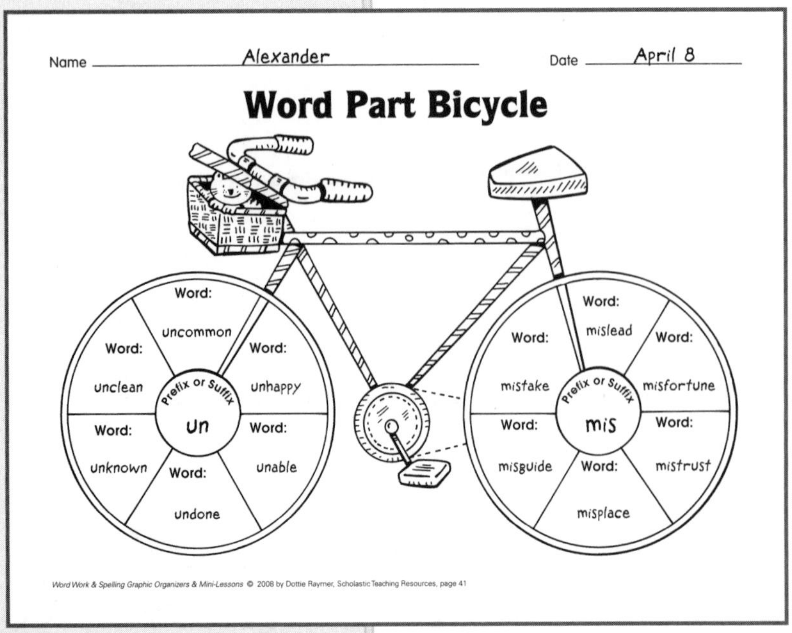

Name Alexander
Date April 8
Word Part Bicycle
Word: uncommon
Word: unhappy
Word: unable
Word: undone
Word: unknown
Word: unclean
Prefix or Suffix
un
Word: mislead
Word: misfortune
Word: mistrust
Word: misplace
Word: misguide
Word: mistake
Prefix or Suffix
mis
Word Work & Spelling Graphic Organizers & Mini-Lessons © 2008 by Dottie Raymer, Scholastic Teaching Resources, page 41

Taking It Further

Ask students to write a prefix or suffix on each wheel on the organizer. Then have them fill in the wheels with words they encounter during reading activities.

Name ______________________________ Date ______________

Word Part Bicycle

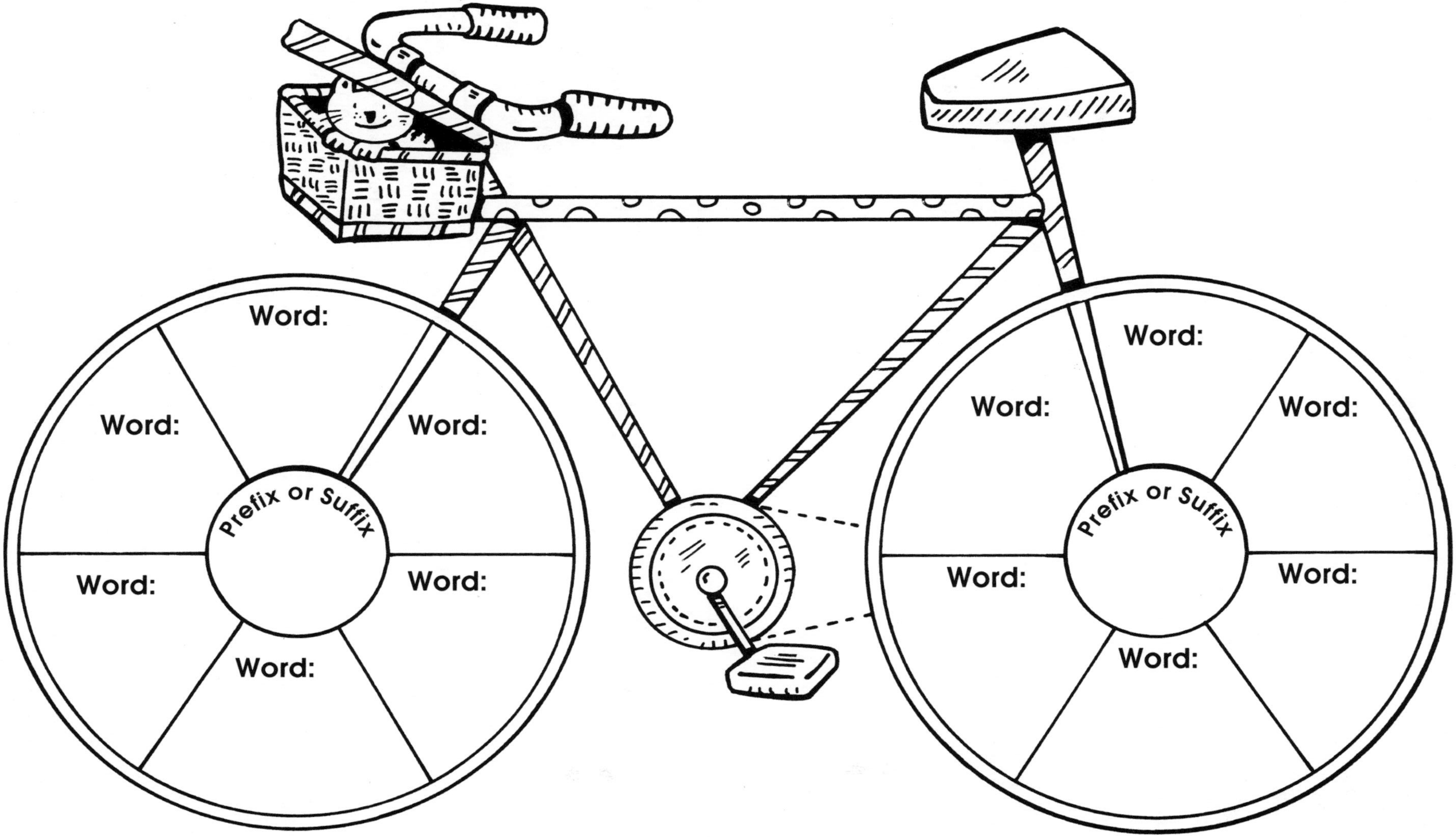
Word:
Word:
Word:
Prefix or Suffix
Word:
Word:
Word:
Word:
Word:
Word:
Prefix or Suffix
Word:
Word:
Word:

Skill

- Understanding Relationships Among Words
- Recognizing Roots and Affixes

Management Tip

After demonstrating how to use this organizer, have students work in small groups to brainstorm words that come from a common root.

Literature Link

Enduring Wisdom: Sayings from Native Americans by Virginia Driving Hawk Sneve (Holiday House, 2003).

The words of wisdom in this collection include sayings from Native Americans, past and present.

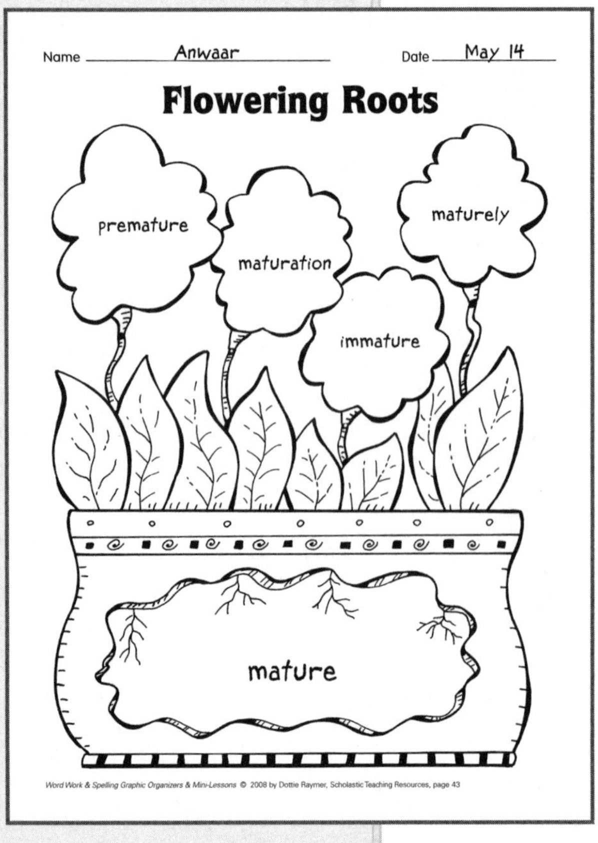

Name Anwaar
Date May 14
Flowering Roots
premature
maturation
maturely
immature
mature
Word Work & Spelling Graphic Organizers & Mini-Lessons © 2008 by Dottie Raymer, Scholastic Teaching Resources, page 43

Flowering Roots

Purpose

Students make meaningful connections between words that contain the same root.

Introducing the Activity

Write *wise* on the board. Ask students to name words that come from this word. They might suggest words such as *wisdom, unwise, otherwise,* and *wisely.* Write their responses above *wise.* Then draw a line from *wise* to each word above it, explaining that this word is the root of the words they named. Ask a volunteer to circle the part of each word that represents the root and note whether or not the spelling is the same as the original word. Afterward, tell students they can use this common word part as a starting point to help them remember how to spell other words that stem from the same root.

Using the Graphic Organizer

1. On the board, write a word that can be used to make 3–4 additional words. For example, you might consider *product (productive, produce, production, reproduction), generate (regenerate, generation, generational, degenerate),* or *mature (premature, maturation, immature, maturely).*
2. Distribute copies of the graphic organizer. Have students copy the word onto the planter.
3. Ask students to brainstorm words that come from the root word. Discuss their responses and list appropriate ones on the board. Have them choose words from the list to write on the flowers.
4. You might instruct students to circle the part of each word on a flower that indicates it comes from the root on the planter. Invite them to tell how that part of the word differs from the original word and identify word parts that were added to create the new word.
5. Provide additional copies of the organizer and a different root word for students to use to complete the activity.

Taking It Further

Challenge students to find their own root words to use to complete the organizer.

Name ______________________________ Date ______________

Flowering Roots

Skill

* Using Spelling Strategies
* Recognizing Spelling Patterns
* Analyzing Word Structure

Management Tip

Invite students to work with partners or in small groups to complete this organizer. Encourage them to share ideas and background knowledge.

Literature Link

Will You Sign Here, John Hancock? by Jean Fritz (PaperStar, 1997).

A biographical account of the life of John Hancock, the first signer of the Declaration of Independence.

Word World

Purpose

Students explore various strategies to help them remember word spellings.

Introducing the Activity

Explain that good spellers often use a variety of strategies to learn how different words are spelled. Then review some strategies that students might try to help them remember the spelling of a word:

* listen to the sounds in a word (phonics)
* notice familiar word parts (word structure)
* look for spelling patterns (visual memory)
* think about the word meaning (spelling-meaning principle)

Using the Graphic Organizer

1. Distribute copies of the graphic organizer. Then choose a word that may be unfamiliar to students but can be found in a text they are reading.
2. Have students write the word on the star. Ask: *What do you notice about this word?* Encourage them to make connections to what they already know about the word. For example, they might brainstorm other words that sound or look like it, that contain parts with a similar spelling, or that look similar and have a related meaning.
3. Instruct students to write words that support their observations on the corresponding planets. Then have them share and explain their responses. For instance, they might explain why *sign* and *signature* have related meanings.
4. As students share, note connections that might be especially useful in helping them remember the word's spelling or meaning. For example, you might point out that the pronunciation of *signature* may help students remember to include the silent g when spelling the related word *sign*.

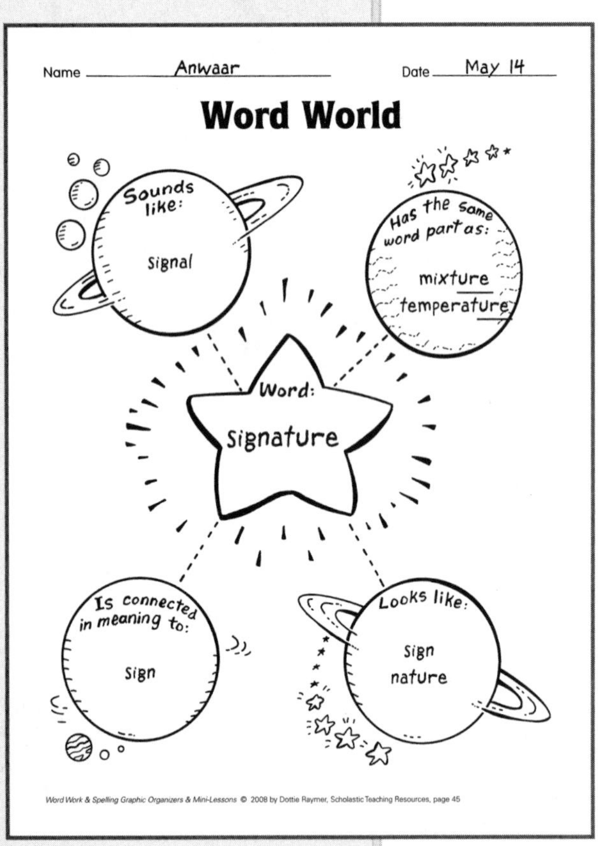

Name Anwaar
Date May 14
Word World
Sounds like:
Signal
Has the same word part as:
mixture
temperature
Word:
Signature
Is connected in meaning to:
Sign
Looks like:
Sign
nature
Word Work & Spelling Graphic Organizers & Mini-Lessons © 2008 by Dottie Raymer, Scholastic Teaching Resources, page 45

Taking It Further

Allow students to draw additional lines and planets on the organizer to record more observations about the word—or other words that share its structure, sound, or meaning.

Name ______________________ Date ______________

Word World

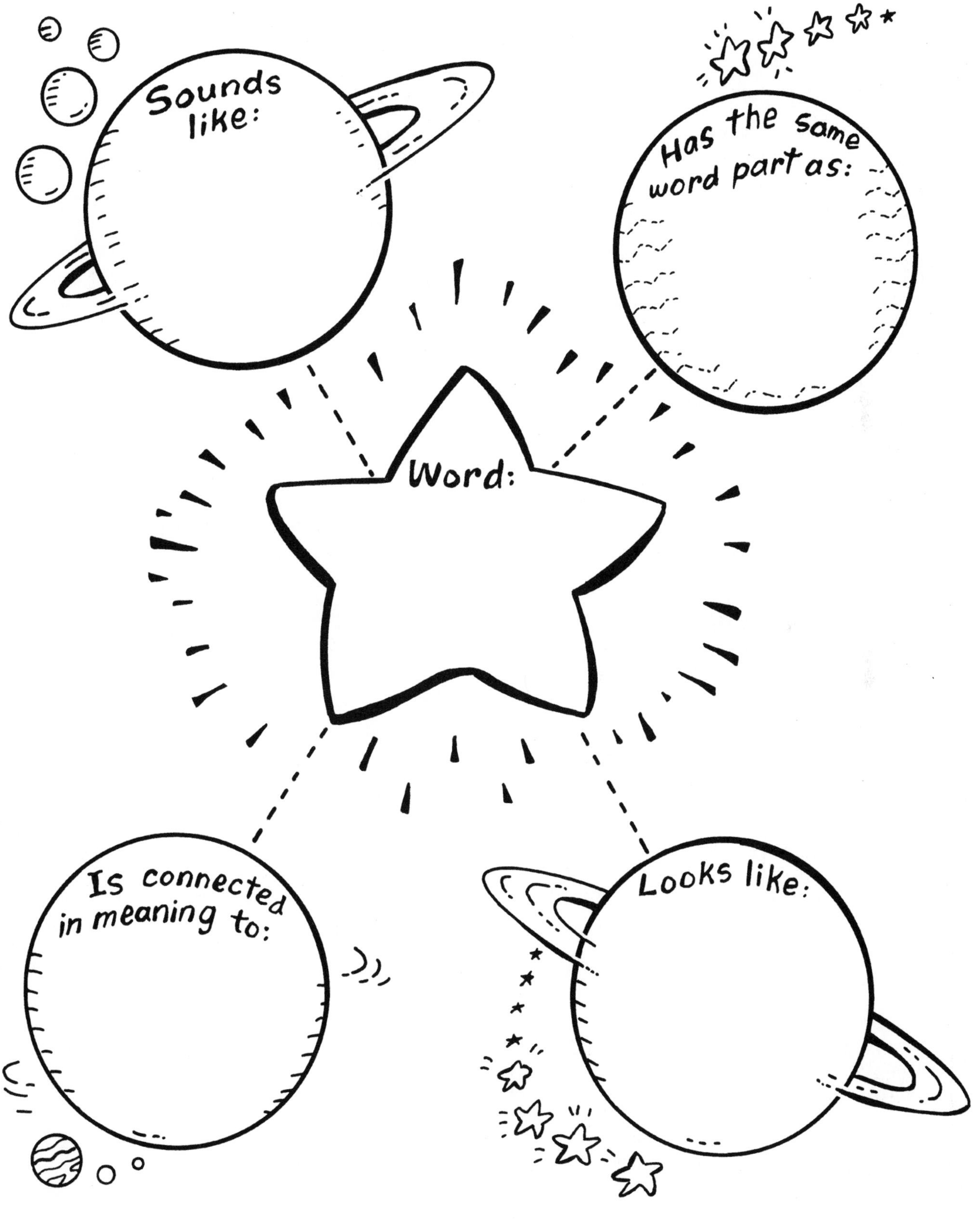

Sounds like:
Has the same word part as:
Word:
Is connected in meaning to:
Looks like:

Skill

- Examining Word Structure
- Recognizing Prefixes, Suffixes, and Roots

Management Tip

Model how to use this organizer on the overhead projector. Display or pass out copies of the chart on page 48 for students to use during the mini-lesson and when completing the organizer independently.

Literature Link

Invisible Stanley by Jeff Brown (HarperTrophy, 2003).

Although Stanley Lambchop is invisible, he keeps busy "showing up" to help others in need.

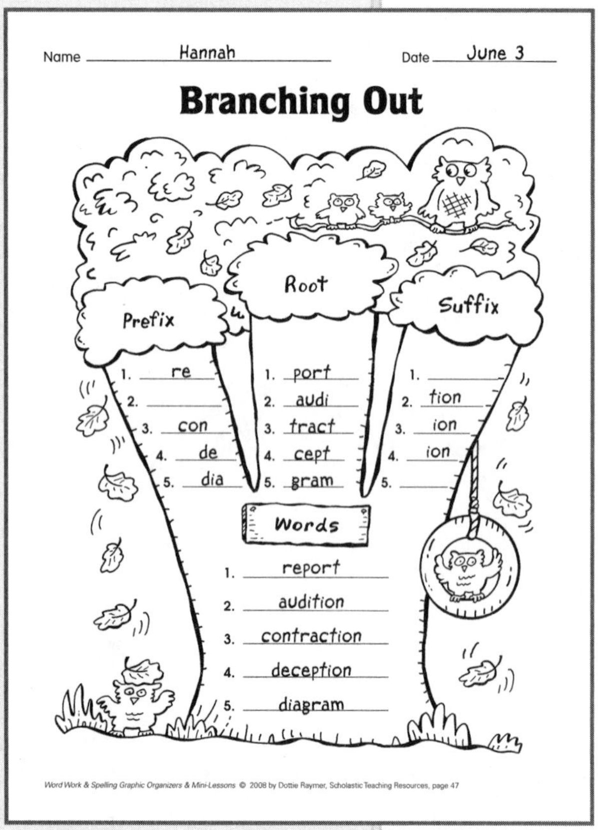

Name Hannah
Date June 3
Branching Out
Root
Prefix
Suffix
1. re
2.
3. con
4. de
5. dia
1. port
2. audi
3. tract
4. cept
5. gram
1.
2. tion
3. ion
4. ion
5.
Words
1. report
2. audition
3. contraction
4. deception
5. diagram
Word Work & Spelling Graphic Organizers & Mini-Lessons © 2008 by Dottie Raymer, Scholastic Teaching Resources, page 47

Branching Out

Purpose

Students separate words into roots, prefixes, and suffixes to explore their spellings and meanings.

Introducing the Activity

Display or pass out copies of the chart on page 48. Then write *transportation* on the board. Explain that many words, like this one, are composed of Latin or Greek roots, prefixes, and suffixes. Ask students to use the chart to help them separate the word into its component parts: *trans* (prefix), *port* (root), and *ation* (suffix). Discuss the meaning of each word part and how it contributes to the full meaning of the word. Tell students that familiarity with the spelling and meaning of a variety of roots, prefixes, and suffixes can help strengthen their spelling skills.

Using the Graphic Organizer

1. Choose a word that contains a Latin or Greek root and at least one prefix or suffix. Write the word on the tree trunk on the graphic organizer.
2. Have students use the chart (page 48) to separate the word into its component parts, writing each part on the corresponding branch (root, prefix, suffix).
3. Talk about the word's spelling and how it relates to the spelling of each of its parts. Discuss how the parts help determine the meaning of the word.
4. Write a different word on each line on the trunk and repeat steps 2 and 3 for each one. Here are some words you might use (see page 48 for more words):

audition	dictation	invisible
biology	hyperactive	position
contraction	immobile	predict
deduction	impossible	reject
dialogue	interception	subtraction

5. Distribute copies of the organizer for students to complete independently or in pairs.

Taking It Further

Have students create words using prefixes, roots, and suffixes from the chart (page 48) and then check the spelling and meaning of each in a dictionary.

Name ________________________________ Date ________________

Branching Out

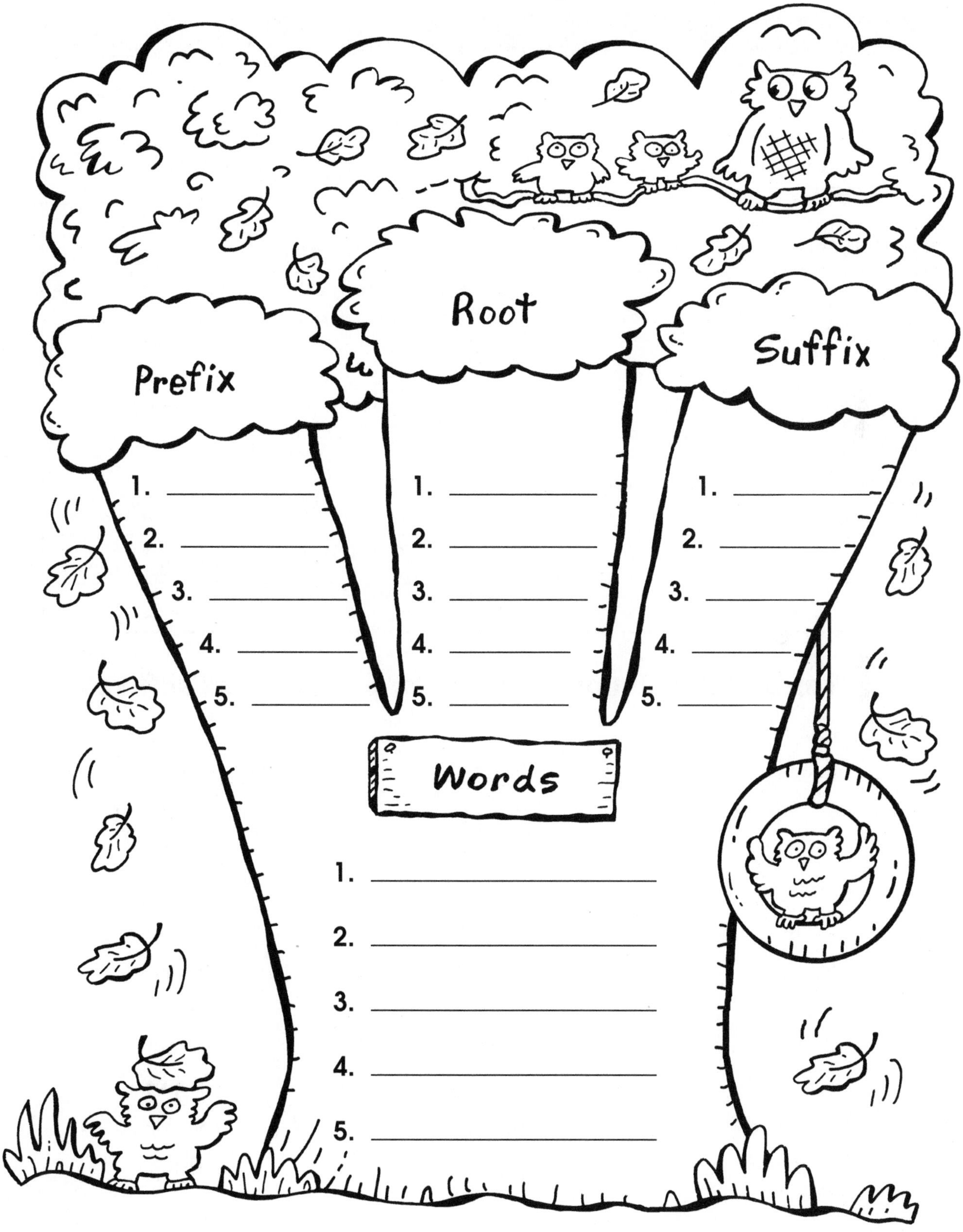
Root
Prefix
Suffix
1. ______
2. ______
3. ______
4. ______
5. ______
1. ______
2. ______
3. ______
4. ______
5. ______
1. ______
2. ______
3. ______
4. ______
5. ______
Words
1. ______
2. ______
3. ______
4. ______
5. ______

Latin and Greek Prefixes, Roots, and Suffixes

Prefix		Root		Suffix
co-, com-, con- *(with or together)*	il-, im-, in-, ir *(not)*	act *(to act)*	meter *(measure)*	-able, -ible *(can be)*
de- *(away, down, off)*	inter- *(among, between)*	audi *(hear)*	mit, mis *(to send)*	-ile *(capable of)*
dia- *(through, across)*	non- *(not)*	auto *(self)*	mot, mov, mob *(to move)*	-ion, -ation *(action or process)*
dis- *(not, not any)*	pre-, pro- *(before, forward)*	bio *(life)*	port *(carry)*	-ity *(condition or quality of)*
de- *(to remove or deduce)*	re- *(again, back)*	cept, ceive, ceipt *(to take, hold)*	pos, posit *(to place, put)*	-ive, -itive *(state of)*
em-, en- *(in)*	sub- *(below, less than)*	dict *(speak)*	rupt *(break)*	-logue, -log *(to speak)*
hyper- *(too much)*	trans- *(across)*	duce, duct *(lead or bring)*	sens, sent *(to feel)*	-logy, -ology *(the study of)*
		erg *(work)*	spec *(to see)*	-ment *(state of being)*
		graph, gram *(write)*	tract *(pull or drag)*	-ous *(full of)*
		ject *(throw)*	vis *(see)*	-sion, -tion *(state or quality)*
				-y *(made up of)*

Words with Latin or Greek roots, prefixes, and suffixes

action
autograph
automobile
biography
concept
conduct
deport
diagram
diameter
dismiss
disruptive
distraction
emerge
enact
energy
hypersensitive
immobile
inspection
interact
interject
interrupt
nonsense
produce
project
reaction
receive
remission
report
sensible
sensitive
subject
submit
transmit
transportation
visible
vision